YESTERDAY, TODAY, and TOMORROW...

"Looking at where Puerto Rico has come from, and seeing the distance she has traveled in comparison with her Caribbean neighbors, it is hard not to be an optimist. All we have to judge anything by is the past ... and judging by the past, Puerto Rico can and will solve her problems. Whatever path Puerto Rico chooses, she will have a future—and most probably a good one!"

—MORTON J. GOLDING

MENTOR and SIGNET Books
of Special Interest

A Short History
of
PUERTO RICO

By
MORTON J. GOLDING

With an Introduction by
LUIS QUERO–CHIESA

A MENTOR BOOK
NEW AMERICAN LIBRARY
TIMES MIRROR
NEW YORK AND SCARBOROUGH, ONTARIO
THE NEW ENGLISH LIBRARY LIMITED, LONDON

F
1971
.G64
1973

 MENTOR TRADEMARK REG. U.S. PAT. OFF. AND FOREIGN COUNTRIES
REGISTERED TRADEMARK—MARCA REGISTRADA
HECHO EN CHICAGO, U.S.A.

SIGNET, SIGNET CLASSICS, SIGNETTE, MENTOR AND PLUME BOOKS
are published *in the United States* by
The New American Library, Inc.,
1301 Avenue of the Americas, New York, New York 10019,
in Canada by The New American Library of Canada Limited,
81 Mack Avenue, Scarborough, 704, Ontario,
in the United Kingdom by The New English Library Limited,
Barnard's Inn, Holborn, London, E.C. 1, England

FIRST PRINTING, MAY, 1973
    1 2 3 4 5 6 7 8 9

PRINTED IN THE UNITED STATES OF AMERICA

For Pat

CONTENTS

Preface

This is a "popular" history written for both the student and the general reader. It is not a textbook in the formal sense, nor is it a scholarly dissertation by a professional historian. If it can interest a few readers in going beyond its own scope by looking into more specialized works, I for one will consider it a success.

Yet even the most modest history book has a responsibility to be accurate as to facts. I have done my best to fulfill this responsibility, although there were times—when two or more sources disagreed on specific dates, for example—when error could only be avoided with a good deal of luck. I can only hope that as few inaccuracies as possible crept into the text, and I apologize for these in advance.

Whatever worth this book has, it would have had far less without the help of a good many people. While it would not be practical to list most of these, there are a few whom I must specifically thank.

First of all, there is Robert Schoene, formerly of the Puerto Rican Information Service, now with the Hotel Association in San Juan. It was Bob Schoene who first suggested to me that I might take on this project. Later, he gave unstintingly of his advice and help. If it were not for his aid in San Juan, much that I was able to accomplish there could not have been done.

Mr. Walter Murray Chiesa, of the Instituto de Cultura Puertorriqueña, spent the better part of one morning answering my questions concerning the Taino Indians. My discussion of the Tainos in this book owes a great deal to him, and I hope that he will not be too dissatisfied with the result.

Dr. Arturo Morales Carrión, a most distinguished historian and author and a member of the History Department of the University of Puerto Rico, took time from his busy schedule to give me suggestions and advice in my research. I owe him a great debt.

I also owe an enormous debt to Dr. Eugenio Fernández Méndez of the University of Puerto Rico, who spent far more time with me than I deserved and then was gracious enough to allow me to photostat his personal bibliography. Dr. Fernández Méndez' latest work, *Historia Cultural de Puerto Rico,* has just been published in San Juan. It would be good if an English edition were soon made available in the United States.

And, of course, I must thank my wife, who has been of more help than she knows—or perhaps than she wanted to be. If it were not for her cooperation in every phase of the preparation of this book—from collecting research material to making telephone calls to reading the entire text—I would most likely still be on Chapter Three or Four. If the result is good it is *our* book; if not, mine.

As for the others who have helped me, I will have to content myself with a general thanks.

MORTON J. GOLDING

A Note on Spanish Names

English-speaking readers are often confused by the Spanish custom—also followed in Puerto Rico—of using two last names. When this occurs, however, the explanation is quite simple: The mother's family name is used in addition to the father's, but is placed at the end. Thus, in this book, the reader will find that the son of Luis Muñoz Rivera is called Luis Muñoz Marín. He may be addressed, incidentally, as either Mr. Muñoz Marín or Mr. Muñoz; but *never* as Mr. Marín.

Introduction

The history of a country—even a popular history—must be more than a horizontal narration of facts and events relating to that country throughout the years. It must shed light upon that intangible, cumulative process that in interplay with events produces the culture of a people. In the case of Puerto Rico that process is most provocative, especially in the light of our present preoccupation with ethnicity and cultures.

What evolves from a reflective study of Puerto Rican history is the human saga of a small island, seemingly doomed to insignificance by history and geography, which has struggled heroically to develop its own personality under the successive influence of two great, absorbent, diametrically opposed cultures. That it has succeeded is evidenced by the fact that Puerto Rican culture *is* different from the Hispanic culture whence it originated and by the stubborn resistance to change which it has shown to the pressure of American culture. Spanish is still the language of the island after three-quarters of a century of American domination, and the physiognomy of its people remains fiercely Puerto Rican.

On November 19, 1493, during his second trip to the New World, Columbus discovered the island—called *Boluchen* in the Indian tongue—and gave it the pious name of San Juan Bautista. After a two-day rest from the long journey across the Atlantic, he replenished his ships with fresh water from the Culebrinas River and continued on his way, putting the small island out of his mind amidst his plans to reach the fabulous Orient. Little did he know that Puerto Rico was to be the last happy moment of that fateful trip which began in splendor and ended in disaster. Nevertheless, the island became a dot on the map of the

Indies and its tradition as a point of hospitality and refreshment had been established. Ponce de León later became its first governor and colonizer, and our first emigrant to what was to be the United States when he left the peace and security of his Caparra home to sail in search of the Fountain of Youth in the Everglades of Florida.

The first Spaniards to occupy the island were the conquistadors, who, like all conquerors, proceeded to establish their own way of life on the conquered land. The often repeated picture of the cross and the sword rising victorious over the indigenous civilization was realized in Puerto Rico in less than a century, with the difference that this time the ruins did not even appear in the picture. With few traces of the indigenous culture left to us, we must penetrate deeper into the history of the island in our search for the origin of Puerto Rican culture.

Cut off from the routes that led to the gold of Peru and the silver of Mexico, Puerto Rico became a fortress at the entrance of the Caribbean Sea—a fortress from which Spain could guard its possessions in that basin. Throughout the first three centuries of its history Puerto Rico was to serve a double purpose as both bastion and point of acclimatization for soldiers, public servants, and slaves destined for other areas of Spanish discovery and colonization in America. These people in transit left the sediment of their cultures on the island without actually determining the character of the Puerto Rican way of life. The chantings coming from the "Slaves Deposit" in the bay of San Juan had little meaning to the inhabitants of the city, which was isolated from outside life by the magnificent walls of its fortifications.

The beginnings were precarious. The island offered little to the immigrants. There was no gold or silver; the jungle did not yield arable land; storms, earthquakes, and pirates plagued life; and mosquitos, fever, and wild ants harassed those who ventured outside the city walls. Yet immigrants came: Andalusians with their guitars, taciturn Basques, sturdy Canary Islanders, Corsican tillers of the land, French scientists, English adventurers, Italian craftsmen. To face the adversities of the environment, they developed their own survival faith. The Festivals of the Cross protected them from earthquakes, and St. Barbara, who held in her hand the cup of the storms, was called on to ward off hurricanes. Meanwhile, the great fires of *tabonuco* kept away the wild ants, and dysentery saved the inhabitants from the English invaders. Slowly Puerto Ricans learned that art of fighting life which they call *la pelea monga* ("the limp fight"), which consists in lying low while the enemy spends himself in furious attack.

The island was governed by captains-general who brought with them royal orders which became royal only after they stamped on them their own imprimatur. There was incessant censorship, and there were attitudes represented by the famous phrase of Governor Pezuela: "Education has ruined the Americas." There was something cruel and degrading called slavery; there were few books, fewer teachers, and no universities. In short, there was everything that could hinder the free development of education and culture. But there was, also, the slow but inevitable gestation of a new kind of man.

The Conquistador—always ready to shed his blood in defense of his honor or to mix it with that of a beautiful native maiden—contributed *hidalguismo*—idealism and flamboyance; the Indian added a drop of pride, and the black man supplied fortitude and fatalism. This was the Puerto Rican formula that was inscribed in the ethnology of America.

Thus, by the nineteenth century there already existed a Puerto Rican man. He may officially be called a "Spaniard from this side of the Atlantic," but he was very different from the "Peninsulars." Black or white, mestizo or mulatto, in his character were present—besides the Spaniard, the Indian, and the Negro—the scenery, the climate, and the colonial insular ambience of the island. He was a man who had already brought new voices to the language and who had transformed the Spanish guitar into a half a dozen new string instruments which he accompanied with the Indian "guiro" and the African drum in a new kind of music—the *seis*, the *bomba*, the *cadenas*—of his own invention. In sum, here was a man who, while he tried to imitate the Madrid fashions and the European style of life, consciously or unconsciously was molding his own culture.

Once the Puerto Rican man defined himself, his creative work was soon to appear, and in the nineteenth century arts and letters were born and acquired their first Puerto Rican identity. Spain sent us a handful of educated and humanistic men who helped condition the environment for the incubation of our culture: Don Luis Paret, chamber painter for King Charles IV, exiled to Puerto Rico, shared his knowledge with José Campeche, a mestizo born in 1752 who was to become the island's first great painter; don José Rodríguez y Calderón, an adventurous Spaniard, brought the first printing press to Puerto Rico; the *intendente* Alejandro Ramírez not only set our economy in order, opened the island's ports to world commerce, and founded a newspaper, but he also established the *Sociedad Económica de Amigos del País* (Economic Society of Friends of Puerto Rico), which for many years fostered the development of sciences, letters, and arts; Father Rufo Manuel Fernández and the Esculapian fathers from the schools of Catalonia began the first secondary-education system, which was to give us a generation of solid and ample culture. The printing press gave us our first newspapers, and there began to appear—often anonymously—the first Puerto Rican literary creations. After that, literature followed a zigzagging course, harassed by censorship, caught in the ebbing of the turbulent history of Spain of those years.

This was also a century of historical contradictions, marking our people's desperate struggle to establish their own personality. It opened with the meeting of the Spanish Cortes in Cádiz, where a Puerto Rican delegate was appointed vice-president, and closed with the second conquest of the island by the American forces. It includes social victories of the caliber of the abolition of slavery in 1873 and the humiliating "compontes" of 1887 when Puerto Rican patriots were imprisoned and tortured for their liberal ideas. It was a century terrible and magnificent at once: everything came to us, and yet, we lacked everything. We got the printing press, but there was no freedom of expression; our ports were opened to maritime traffic, but commerce was in the hands of foreigners; the island was opened to universal culture but was denied its own university. Spain, as her empire crumbled in America, tried obstinately to prolong her stay by holding on desperately to Cuba and Puerto Rico. Her internal troubles were so demanding that she could not focus on the problems in America, and Cuba and Puerto Rico remained at the mercy of their captains-general—little despots, with honorable exceptions, who had a tendency to confuse the legitimate aspirations of the people with treason, and fear-based adulation with loyalty.

Despite these contradictions, by the end of the nineteenth century Puerto Rico could proudly present a roster of distinguished writers and artists. There were thinkers of the quality of Eugenio María de Hostos and Matienzo Cintrón;

poets like José Gautier Benítez and Lola Rodríguez de Tió; novelists of the stature of Alejandro Tapia and Manuel Zeno Gandía; newspapermen of the agility and incisiveness of Luis Muñoz Rivera and Mariano Abril; jurists like Jacinto Texidor y Calderón; historians like Cayetano Coll y Toste and Salvador Brau; and playwrights as talented as Ramón Méndez Quiñones, to mention but a few who are worthy of the attention of future scholars who wish to probe more deeply into the history and development of Puerto Rican culture.

In view of the continuing oppression and neglect by the Spaniards during the four centuries they ruled Puerto Rico, one may wonder why the Puerto Ricans did not take up arms against the Spanish on the same scale as had taken place throughout Latin America in the first half of the nineteenth century, and which recurred intermittently in Cuba during the last quarter of the century. The particular circumstances of Puerto Rico and the culture that had developed there, however, led the majority of Puerto Ricans to prefer autonomy within a Spanish sphere to outright independence from the mother country. Nineteenth-century Puerto Rican leaders such as Muñoz Rivera fought to establish rights for the islanders equal to those of Spanish citizens of the peninsula. By the time of the outbreak of the 1898 war between the United States and Spain, Muñoz had succeeded in setting up a commonwealth relationship with Spain. Nevertheless, events in Cuba and Washington turned history in another direction for Puerto Rico.

In July of 1898 the American army landed in Puerto Rico. Puerto Rican life was profoundly affected by the arrival of the United States forces. A new culture had suddenly descended upon us. Its values were alien to our hispanic way of life, and by the same token, the new power could not understand some of our natural postures.

Caught in the confusion of that encounter, Puerto Rico started to feel its way in a new direction. Madrid was no longer the goal of our pilgrimage. Providence had moved to Washington.

The Puerto Ricans soon learned to accept what was useful from American culture while at the same time persisting in the development of their own. Under American influence, modern Puerto Rico has produced a host of creative artists and intellectuals, significant men of action, an increasingly large educated middle class, and a multitude of skilled workers. The island continues to be the point of contact for the United States with Latin America, and its scholars, journalists, and businessmen make important contributions in this area. Meanwhile, the jet transport has brought Puerto Rican intellectuals and writers in contact with the main currents of art and ideas.

Buttressed by our own cultural values and encouraged by American generosity, the Puerto Rican people face the future with faith in themselves, conscious of their failures and achievements. Before them lies a world in which atomic energy remedies the lack of natural resources and smallness is measured in terms of intellectual deficiency.

As a chronicle of historical events that have helped shape the lives of Puerto Ricans up to now, Mr. Golding's *Short History of Puerto Rico* is an excellent work. I share with him the desire that larger numbers of English-speaking readers will dig deeply into the human factors surrounding those events. They will certainly find a continuum of warm, creative, and persevering people who are proud of their history and culture, notwithstanding their suffering, calamities, and deprivation.

—Luis Quero-Chiesa
January 1973

Editor's note: Luis Quero-Chiesa was born in Puerto Rico and received his early education there. After attending the Parsons School of Design in New York City and struggling through the Depression years, he eventually became vice-president of a major firm in advertising and public relations. In addition to pursuing his interest in Puerto Rican culture, he has played an active role in civic affairs, and in 1971 he was appointed Chairman of the Board of Higher Education of the City of New York.

ONE

BEGINNINGS

The real story has its start far back in time with a land mass—a great island or small continent—located in what is now the Caribbean area and extending all the way west to modern Central America and beyond. It was about a hundred million years ago (give or take a few million) that volcanic activity caused the greater part of this mysterious land mass to sink into the water.

This was not the end of it, however. The land mass was to have a second life during a later geologic period.

One of the characteristics of the reborn continent was its lofty mountain ranges. Some of the peaks rose to towering heights of more than twenty thousand feet above sea level. And when the land mass sank back into the sea once more, certain peaks and ranges were to remain above the water.

Among the different bodies of land formed in this way were the Greater Antilles, a group of islands which includes Jamaica, Cuba, Hispaniola, and Puerto Rico—which is the smallest of the four.

Puerto Rico is approximately one hundred miles long and thirty-five miles wide, with a roughly rectangular shape. Within these confines there are marked contrasts. The island can boast both rain forests and dry, arid patches. It has low coastal plains and valleys along with mountains that range up to four thousand feet. The variety of plant life is enormous, but there are few indigenous mammals.

Man is one of the mammals that is not indigenous to Puerto Rico. Man came late.

Who were the first Puerto Rican men and women? They most likely belonged to a primitive group of Indians known as the Siboney.

They lived on whatever the land provided and depended mainly on fruit and marine life for their sustenance. It is not possible to say precisely when they came to the Greater Antilles. The end of their control, however, was signaled in about 700 A.D., when a new group of Indians started to arrive in the area.

This was the far more highly civilized Taino group. Wherever the Tainos landed in the Caribbean, they easily overcame and pushed back the Siboney. And by the year 1270 they had taken over the island which they called Boriquén: present-day Puerto Rico.

The Tainos were members of a large family of West Indian and South American Indians, all the members of which spoke related languages. The Spanish gave this family their name of Arawak.

Although traces of the Arawaks have been found as far south as the tropical sections of Argentina, the Tainos themselves probably came from Venezuela and spread northward into the Caribbean. They were a basically peaceful, agrarian people who came to settle and not merely to raid.

While the Taino culture was not as spectacular as that of the Mayans of the Yucatan, for example, it was a huge advance over Siboney's civilization. In Boriquén, as in other islands where they settled, the Tainos produced a kind of bread from the yucca plant, grew vegetables such as corn and yams, and manufactured cotton cloth. They were also skilled in the arts, creating fine pottery which they decorated with the symbolic head of their major god—a deity with the imposing name of Yocahu Vagua Maorocoti. Yocahu's stylized features may also be seen on large flat stones which the Tainos carved with loving care.

The Tainos lived in wooden framed huts with thatched roofs. These huts bear a resemblance to the dwelling places of members of the much greater Indian civilizations (such as the Mayan) which flourished in Central and South America. Another point of resemblance is the ceremonial ball game that was ubiquitous among early American civilizations.

Taino ball courts—or *bateys*, as they were called in Boriquén—are now being investigated on the island. At these Puerto Rican sites are found the three-pointed stone idols known as *cemis* and the ceremonial stone collars that are typical of the Taino civilization wherever it flourished.

The gentle Tainos lived an almost paradisiacal existence on their bountiful island of Boriquén. Under the political rule of their supreme chief, or *cacique*, and spiritually guided by their medicine man, or *bujiti*, they created a life for themselves in which they had to work a mere five hours a day.

There was, however, a serpent in this paradise—one which cast a shadow over the entire world of the Tainos. This was another group of Indians called the Caribs.

The Caribs, who lent their name to the entire area, were as bloodthirsty and warlike as the Tainos were peaceful. They came originally from the northern section of South America and took over the Lesser Antilles from the Tainos. From those bases, they carried out long-distance raids on Taino settlements to the north.

Despite the contemptuous terms in which they were described by certain early Spanish writers, the Tainos were not a cowardly people. They fought bravely to defend themselves from Carib raiders. But the Taino short spear, with a point made from fire-hardened wood or the teeth of fish, was no match for the more sophisticated bows and arrows of the fierce Caribs.

The raids took terrible tolls—and not just in life. The Caribs would come to Boriquén in their great dugout canoes to burn and to sack, and especially to take back captives.

The Caribs used these captives in a particularly horrifying way. Young Taino male prisoners were castrated, fed until they were fat, and then ritually eaten. The word "cannibal" comes from Carib, derived from the word "Caribal."

Thus it was in Boriquén: A pleasant life for the most part, but frightfully punctuated by the terrifying Carib raids. Then, on the night of November 18, 1493, that life came to a sudden end. For on that night a fleet of seventeen vessels sailed up to the island.

On the following morning, the natives could see the fleet for themselves. To their eyes, the ships must have been enormous—far larger than even the feared Carib dugouts. They could not know it, of course, but the fleet had sailed all the way from Spain. And in command was the Italian-born navigator Christopher Columbus.

In that year, 1493, Columbus was at the height of his fame and influence. In Europe, his name was a word to reckon with. The rulers of Spain themselves had paid him homage. He had already discovered—or so the Western world believed—an inexpensive way to reach the Orient by sea. Few doubted that he would soon find a trade route connecting the West with the fabulous court of the Great Khan which Marco Polo had so vividly described some two hundred years before.

And an ocean trade route was badly wanted. By now, the Renaissance was in full swing. Europe was changing from a feudal to a mercantile society. New horizons were opening up in art and literature, in philosophy, in political theory and practice, and—not least of all—in trade. The age of imperialism, with all its attendant benefits and evils, was anxious to be born.

Columbus was a child of his times. Born in Genoa, he was the son of a successful weaver and was probably trained in boyhood to follow that craft. A few centuries earlier, that would have been the end of it. He would have ended his days satisfied that he had followed in his father's footsteps. But the world was changing. When Columbus was fourteen years old, he went to sea.

Columbus spent his youth on the water. He experienced sea battles, at least one major shipwreck, and in the year 1477, he sailed to Iceland. This country, incidentally, had once owned a colony in Greenland. It kept in touch with the colony for more than four hundred years and only lost contact with it in the early fifteenth century. So it is very possible that Columbus learned in Iceland that there was indeed a land which lay beyond "ultima Thule."

But although Columbus had more than his share of adventures, he was not a simple adventurer. He was both a merchant and a ship's captain. His family connections were not to be sneered at, either. After settling in Portugal, he married a girl from one of the most important noble families in that kingdom.

Columbus was a religious man. And although not a scholar, he did take an interest in classical writings. His dream of making a great voyage across the western ocean, in fact, was probably influenced more by his readings in ancient literature and the Bible than by science or any tales he might have picked up in Iceland.

One Biblical passage which helped inspire his enterprise can be found in Isaiah 11: 10-12. This tells of a time when the Lord will recover "the remnant of His people ... from the islands of the sea" and "gather together the dispersed of Judah from the four corners of the earth." Columbus was also impressed by a section in the play *Medea,* by the first century (A.D.) Roman writer Seneca, who foresaw an age when "the Ocean will loose the chains of things, and a huge land lie revealed. . . ."

The present-day legend of Columbus as the only man of his generation who realized that the earth is round, is untrue. Only the most primitive or unlettered men of that time believed in the flat-earth theory. The great scientific philosophers of ancient Greece and Rome—such as Aristotle, for example, or Ptolemy—knew very well that the earth is round. When the poet Dante wrote his *Divine Comedy* in the early fourteenth century, he pictured the earth as a sphere. The learned men of Columbus' era also understood that fact.

Columbus' problem, then, was not to convince the people he dealt with that it could be *theoretically* possible to reach the Orient by sailing westward. There was no argument about that. He had to prove it to be a *practical* scheme in terms of current ships and navigational aids. A crew should not have to spend an impossibly long time at sea, for instance.

Columbus tried to answer the objections of his critics by showing that the globe was smaller and the ocean narrower than anyone had thought. Actually he was wrong in this. His calculations were about 25 per cent off. But by using them, he was able to convince both himself and many others that a voyage to the land of the Great Khan was practical.

There were still more, however, whom he could not convince. In 1488 Columbus approached the court of King John II of Portugal with the idea of convincing that monarch to be his sponsor. King John appointed a committee of mathematicians to deal with the matter, and the committee came out strongly against any royal sponsorship of Columbus' projected voyage. It reached this conclusion not because its members believed in a flat earth, but because they disagreed (correctly) with Columbus' calculations regarding the size of the earth.

It was after this rejection in Portugal that Columbus went to Spain.

At the time, Spain was not a single political unity. It was two political entities in the process of becoming united by their respective monarchs. The fact that these monarchs were husband and wife was certainly speeding up the process of unification, but this did not mean that the process was complete. Far from it.

Ferdinand II was the king of Aragon with its attendant territories. His wife, Queen Isabella, was the heiress of Henry IV of Castile. Under their marriage contract, the two kingdoms retained their separate laws and political institutions, with Queen Isabella being supreme in Castilian affairs.

When these rulers heard Columbus' proposal—to open up a new trade route to the East in exchange for wealth and honors—they reacted in much the same way as had King John of Portugal. They appointed a committee.

The Spanish committee was under the chairmanship of the highly respected bishop of Avila, Hernando de Talavera. Talavera and the others debated for four years before finally turning Columbus down. In the end, they had to agree with the Portuguese experts.

This was a low point in Columbus' career. He even considered leaving Spain for good. That he changed his mind was largely due to two men whom he had recently met. Martín Alonzo Pinzón, an important ship-owner, agreed to become a partner in the Indies enterprise. Juan Pérez, a friar with influence at the court, helped to get Columbus another royal audience.

The friar must have made a strong impression on Queen Isabella. She not only recalled the navigator, but sent him a sum of money so that he might purchase finer clothing and transportation to the temporary court of Granada.

If the queen was now more interested, however, Columbus' own demands were escalating. He showed up with a list of demands that included a knighthood, and the title of grand admiral and viceroy over any lands he might discover. On top of everything else, he wanted one tenth of the value of whatever might be brought back from such lands—jewels, for example, or spices or precious metals or anything else.

When they heard all this, the king and queen must have winced. But Columbus refused to compromise. The royal couple, therefore, wished him luck and sent him on his way.

Columbus started out for France with every intention of presenting that country with the same offer that Spain had rejected.

On the very day that he left the court, however, the powerful "keeper of the privy purse," Luis de Santangel, was convincing Queen Isabella to change her mind. If Columbus *did* happen to be right—if the ocean *did* turn out to be narrower than anyone else thought—the rewards and glory that Spain would gain through having a trade route to the East would be enormous. Even considering Columbus' inflated demands, the gamble would be worth it. Santangel felt so strongly about it, indeed, that he even offered to advance the money needed to get the expedition under way. As it turned out, this proved unnecessary—just as it was unnecessary for the queen to pawn her jewels.

Three ships were outfitted and made ready: the *Niña,* the *Pinta,* and the *Santa María.* Among the items carried on the ships was a supply of cheap baubles which Columbus could use to trade for gold in case he ran into savages. Also on board was an official linguist—a man proficient in Arabic—who might come in handy if the expedition found the Great Khan.

After a long, eventful voyage, the ships came to the Bahamas, which Columbus mistook for Pacific islands near Japan. There he saw his first Tainos, whom he found both friendly and generous. The Indian name for the first island he reached was Guanahani, meaning "iguana." Columbus renamed the island San Salvador, which is how it is known today.

Although Columbus must have been upset that his official linguist was of little use in communicating with the Indians, he did not let this fact dissuade him from believing that he had reached the Orient. The Indians did wear gold ornaments and, communicating through gestures, they let the Spaniards know that they were terrified of a powerful people who lived on a much larger island. The large island (actually Cuba) had to be Japan, Columbus reasoned.

Taking along some captive Tainos, the admiral led his small fleet through the Bahamas and toward the coast of Cuba. Here too, there were gold objects to be found and friendly Tainos who were willing to help the strangers from across the sea. When the Spaniards asked the Indians where the gold came from, they were answered honestly: "Cubancan"—meaning the central section of Cuba. Columbus, however, took the word to be *"el gran can"*—or the Great Khan—and was even more positive that he was on the right track.

He sent an embassy into the interior with gifts, trading items, and a letter from the rulers of Spain. The embassy came back with a sad report. There was no Oriental court in the center of the island—just a primitive village. There was one interesting item, however. The villagers had introduced the members of the embassy to the first cigar ever smoked by Europeans.

From Cuba, the admiral sailed to another large island which he called Hispaniola, now the home of Haiti and the Dominican Republic. There the *Santa María* ran aground and was lost. Since the *Pinta*, under the command of Martín Alonzo Pinzón, had disappeared in a storm on the way to Hispaniola, Columbus founded a colony with men from the *Santa María* and started home in the *Niña*.

He met the *Pinta* again, and the two ships sailed for Spain, where they arrived separately. The discovery of Puerto Rico was going to have to wait for his second voyage.

Notwithstanding the rivalry which had developed between Martín Alonzo Pinzón and himself, Columbus had the kind of homecoming that he must have dreamed of. He was given wealth, great honor, and an important coat of arms. He also collected the cash reward for being the first man in the expedition to sight land—a reward he did not actually deserve.

He did deserve the other honors, however. If it were not for Columbus' stubborn insistence in his own theories —even when those theories were mistaken—the queen would not have financed the project in the first place, and it is doubtful that Spain herself would have developed into the strong and wealthy colonial power she later became. It can even be argued that the character of Puerto Rico—a character which was largely formed when the island was one of the Caribbean jewels in the crown of Spain—would have turned out to be very different if Columbus had not been the man he was.

No sooner had the first expedition to the Indies returned, in any event, than there was talk about a second.

This was to be larger than the first, with a fleet of seventeen ships instead of three, and Columbus was once more to be in command.

He had already proved—by bringing back samples of gold and other items—that a profit could be made from the Indies. Now he was determined to reach both the court of the Great Khan and the fabled island of Japan, where, according to Marco Polo, the royal palaces were actually roofed with gold.

The fleet made its first landfall on the wooded island of Marie-Galante and then headed for the nearby island of Guadeloupe, where it lay at anchor for six days. It was here that the Spaniards had their first encounter with the hostile Caribs.

Until now, Columbus and his men had encountered only the Taino Indians, and they were full of praise for this gentle people. The Caribs were something new. In a deserted village the shore party found castrated Taino boys who were being fattened to be used as food, and Taino girls who were being used to produce the babies that the Caribs found particularly delicious. Several huts contained actual joints and cuts of human flesh.

The Spaniards were naturally aghast at the sights they saw. Taking about twenty of the captured Tainos with them, they made their way back to the fleet.

When Columbus heard what had happened, he ordered his men to burn all the Carib dugout canoes they could find. He wanted to prevent the cannibals from continuing their raids upon the Tainos, whom he looked upon as his friends.

On leaving Guadeloupe, the fleet sailed north and west, landing first on Nevis and then on an island which Columbus named Santa Cruz, but which is now known by its French translation, St. Croix. Here Columbus sent out another shore party which ran across a group of seven Caribs—four men, two women, and a boy.

Although they were heavily outnumbered and had only bows and arrows to match against Spanish guns, the Caribs put up a furious battle in which they managed to kill one Spaniard and wound another. In the end, the natives were disarmed, captured, and taken back to the fleet. But even then they looked so fierce and warlike that the Spaniards grew nervous merely watching them.

This minor skirmish was the very first engagement between Europeans and the Indians of the New World. As everyone now knows, it was far from the last.

The second battle with the Indians, indeed, followed almost immediately. A whole crowd of Carib warriors advanced to the shore on St. Croix in order to threaten the fleet which was riding at anchor.

The fleet was not really in danger. Carib arrows could not reach it. But the sailors were bothered by the very sight of the warriors, who shaved one half of their heads while letting their hair hang down from the other, and who painted their bodies in many different colors. Columbus apparently decided that he was tempting fate to remain where he was, and the fleet set sail once more.

Later that day, the ships began to sail through a group of about one hundred small islands that Columbus named the Virgin Islands after the story of St. Ursula and her women companions. Two days later, on November 18, the fleet reached the small island of Vieques and then proceeded to a much larger island—the one which the Tainos called Boriquén and which Columbus renamed San Juan Bautista. The story of Puerto Rico had crossed that of Christopher Columbus.

The fleet reached Puerto Rico during the night and probably stood off shore until the following morning. That day, November 19, a strong wind came up to prevent Columbus from landing. He led his ships along the southern coast, therefore, and did not attempt to land until the twentieth, when he rounded the southwest corner of the island and found the peaceful waters of Boquerón Bay.

The fleet remained at anchor in the bay for two days while the men located fresh provisions and water. The Spaniards wanted to trade with the Tainos, but the Indians —apparently taking fright at their approach—disappeared into the interior. A party of men who went in search of the natives found a small but well-planned village complete with central plaza, twelve huts, and one larger house. But the village was empty of people.

On November 22, Columbus and his fleet left Puerto Rico to sail toward Hispaniola, Cuba, and Jamaica. Although Columbus was to sail along the south shore of the island a second time—during his final voyage of discovery, in the summer of 1502—he would never set foot on Puerto Rico again.

This crossing of the path of Puerto Rico's history with that of Christopher Columbus marks the start of the island's life as a Spanish colony. Before discussing that life, however, we should take a brief afterglance at Christopher Columbus.

Ahead of him was the long trip back to Spain and two more voyages of discovery. Although he actually landed on the coast of the South American continent, he would never recognize the fact that he had really discovered a new world and would always regret not finding either Japan or the court of the Great Khan.

Ahead of Columbus, also, were bitter and futile battles with the Spanish court over what he considered to be his proper honors and the money he believed to be due him.

But even though Columbus' personal history was to end in bitterness and frustration, the forces he had set in motion were to continue. The world would never be the same again.

TWO

ISLE OF GOLD

One of the men-at-arms aboard Columbus' fleet which called at Puerto Rico in 1493 was a thirty-three-year-old soldier named Juan Ponce. Ponce came from the kingdom of León (now a province in northwest Spain) and had served with distinction in the wars against the Moors.

Ponce de León, however, was to make his future in the New World. For a number of years he saw service on the island of Hispaniola. Then, in 1508, he asked for and received permission to explore and settle San Juan Bautista.

Ponce was not the first man to obtain permission to settle San Juan. In 1499 Vicente Yáñez Pinzón—commander of the *Niña* on Columbus' first voyage of discovery and brother of Columbus' old partner, Martín Alonzo Pinzón—was given a commission to conquer and colonize the island which was to be called Puerto Rico. But Yáñez Pinzón did not follow through. In 1506—the year of Columbus' death—he transferred his own rights and titles to Martín García de Zalazar.

Although Yáñez Pinzón and Zalazar did manage to land a few goats and hogs on the island, it was still uncolonized in 1508. San Juan was only employed, at that time, as a convenient place for ships to call at in order to pick up fresh provisions.

Spain considered this situation to be wasteful. There was little doubt that the island contained gold.

So Ponce de León set out with a party of fifty men. If gold *was* there, he was determined to find it.

Juan Ponce de León was a *conquistador*—a term which means conqueror. And like the other *conquistadores* of his day, he was not in the business of military conquest merely for the fun of it.

The Spanish *conquistadores* had three major goals in life. As Christians, they hoped to convert the "heathen" Indians to Christianity. As Spaniards, they wanted to bring glory and profit to the Spanish crown. And as men, they hoped to make their own fortunes.

At this distance in time, it is only too easy to be cynical about which of these goals was most important. However, there is little doubt that the vast majority of *conquistadores* were sincere patriots. And even when they did not hesitate to destroy an Indian's body in order to save his soul, they were certainly sincere in their religious beliefs. At the same time, though, it cannot be denied that the idea of making a personal fortune in the Indies was a very important motivation.

The *conquistadores*, indeed, organized their expeditions as risk-taking, profit-making business enterprises. They equipped the expeditions themselves, often going into great debt in order to obtain the necessary money. In return, many of them became men of enormous wealth— even after one fifth of their incomes (the royal *quinto*) was taken by the Spanish crown in taxes.

Even their worst enemies could not accuse the *conquistadores* of laziness when it came to battle. In warfare they did what had to be done. The dull drudgery of manual labor, on the other hand, was something that the average *conquistador* had little taste for. If the jungles were to be cleared, therefore, if gold was to be mined and if crops were to be grown and harvested, a large force of unskilled workers was essential.

The vast majority of Spaniards believed that it was only just for that force to be made up of the native Indians. Were not these savages granted the privilege of being introduced to Christianity? Were they not being slowly guided away from their ignorant savage state and being led toward European-style civilization? Were they not even permitted to become subjects of the king of Spain? The only way the Indians could repay their benefactors, the Spaniards reasoned, was by performing the necessary tasks of humble labor.

The system under which the Indians were led to perform these tasks was developed on the island of Hispaniola by Nicolás de Ovando, who was not only the governor of Hispaniola but the royal governor of all the Indies.

Ovando was sent to Hispaniola in 1502 and ordered to put down a series of rebellions by both the Indians and certain factions among the Spanish themselves. Within one year Ovando had done the job. He had pacified the island, hanged the ruling Indian princess, Anacaona, for treason, and was starting to work out his system of *encomiendas*.

This system had much in common with the feudalism of the Middle Ages—on which it was probably based. Indian lands were chopped up and given to *conquistadores* who were then held responsible for both the actions and the moral state of "their" natives. Their power over the Indians was practically unlimited. Their relationship to them was that of masters to serfs. It was not only the right but the obligation of a Spanish *encomendero* to ensure that the natives under him did the necessary labor.

To a twentieth-century eye, this system appears to be a not very subtle rationalization of slavery. The Spaniards defended it, however, by pointing out the fact that an *encomendero* was held responsible for the religious and moral condition of "his" Indians. In the official view, at least, he was not only an overlord, but something of a missionary who was obligated to lead the Indians to the Christian way of life by teaching and by example.

It will be remembered that Juan Ponce de León spent several years on the island of Hispaniola. As a *conquistador*, therefore, he underwent an apprenticeship under the same Nicolás de Ovando who designed the system of *encomiendas*. And when Ponce applied for permission to settle San Juan Bautista and take over the governorship of that island, it was Ovando who gave him his commission.

Ponce proved an apt pupil. He and his fifty-man team landed on a well-protected bay—later to be called San Juan Bay—which he named Puerto Rico. (Legend has it that he exclaimed, "Oh, what a rich port!"—*"puerto rico"*—as he sailed into the harbor.)

Soon Ponce and his *conquistadores* were putting Ovando's system into practice. Everything went smoothly—so smoothly, in fact, that it began to appear as if Ponce would never need to draw on the military experience he had gathered on Hispaniola and in the war against the Moors.

The *cacique* of the Tainos of Boriquén was a man named Aguebana whose mother—perhaps hearing of the fate of Hispaniola's Princess Anacaona—advised her son to cooperate with the Spaniards. Aguebana followed this advice. Ponce was welcomed and feasted. He even went through a Taino name-exchanging ceremony, in which he and the chief temporarily took each other's name.

It was not long before the first Spanish settlement was built. This was Villa de Caparra, which was located somewhat inland from the shore, opposite the present city of San Juan.

In building this town, Ponce made an error. The site was an unhealthy one, and the Spaniards who lived there were preyed upon by disease. In addition to this, the route to the bay was difficult to traverse. It has been estimated that it cost more money to transport goods from the ships in the harbor to Caparra than it did to ship the goods from Spain in the first place.

In 1519 these factors led the Spaniards to replace Caparra with a new city which they placed on a small island that protected the entrance to the harbor. This new town was a vast success. It grew and spread until it became the thriving metropolis that San Juan is today.

In those early days, however, Ponce de León was not worried about the future of his Caparra. There was gold on the island, and the system of *encomiendas* seemed to be working perfectly. He built a fortified house in Caparra, and in 1509 he proved his faith in the colony by sending for his wife and daughters to join him there.

Ponce had every reason to be sanguine about the future of the island. From all indications, its future seemed certain to be a golden one, both literally and figuratively. That gleaming and valuable metal was there in amounts that startled everyone. As early as 1511, the Spanish court was astounded to receive as much as ten thousand pesos in gold from the mines of San Juan Bautista. Perhaps, Spain speculated happily, the mines there were going to turn out to be even more productive than the mines on Hispaniola.

For a while it seemed as if the Spaniards' wildest dreams were coming true. During the first part of 1515, for example, a new mine was discovered which yielded gold in the value of 25,000 pesos within just a few months. By 1520 the king's share of the island's gold—that is, one fifth of the total—was estimated at about eighty thousand pesos a year.

The island's economy was booming. There was a growing trade with Spain that was only threatened by hurricanes which menaced shipping and by the continuing raids of the Carib Indians from nearby islands.

The Carib raiders were a very severe problem. They came wherever a new settlement was built, burning houses and crops, killing the Spaniards, and carrying off the Tainos as slaves. In 1520 they attacked a new settlement on the banks of the Humacao River, in 1521 they were attacking the southern shore of the island, and in 1529 they were making bold raids against the capital city.

It was not, in fact, until the beginning of the seventeenth century that these Carib raiders were finally put down. Even then, incidentally, they were not defeated by the Spaniards, but by the French and British privateers who were preying on Spain's overseas possessions.

In the beginning, however, the very raids of the Caribs managed to aid San Juan's economic boom. It was in order to intimidate these fierce tribesmen that Spain, in 1510, ordered all of its ships bound *anywhere* in the Indies to make their first stop at San Juan. While the intimidation did not work, this policy did ensure a continual flow of men and new supplies to the settlement.

And the gold kept coming. Between 1509 and 1539 a total of 286,963 pesos of it was transported from San Juan to Seville.

In the meantime, though, Ponce de León was having political troubles.

In 1509 the Spanish crown replaced Ponce's mentor, Nicolás de Ovando, as governor of the Indies. The new man was Christopher Columbus' son, Don Diego Columbus, who promptly decided to remove Ponce as governor of San Juan—despite the fact that King Ferdinand had given him his own appointment with the understanding that Ponce was to stay on.

Don Diego's choice for the job was a man named Juan Cerón. But when Cerón showed up in San Juan, he did not find Ponce in an accepting mood. This was his (Ponce's) territory. And Ponce controlled the chief constable, Cristóbal de Sotomayor. Instead of being installed as governor, Cerón found himself arrested and bundled aboard a ship leaving for Spain.

With this problem temporarily out of the way, at least, Ponce could now concentrate upon another: growing trouble with the Taino Indians.

Perhaps the most surprising thing about the Indian uprising of 1511 is that the Tainos had been as patient as they were, for as long as they were. The natives, who had lived a carefree, almost idyllic existence before the Spaniards came, now found themselves being treated as slaves and forced to work from dawn to sunset in Spanish mines or plantations. Even the vicious Caribs had only enslaved a small percentage of them. The Spanish were oppressing the entire Taino population.

One reason sometimes given for the Tainos' hesitancy to rebel is that they considered the Spaniards to be gods and therefore immortal. This belief, according to the story, was finally exploded when a pair of Tainos killed a Spanish planter and stood guard over his body for two days and nights to learn whether or not he would return to life. He did not.

Regardless of the truth of this tale, it is a fact that the long-suffering Tainos had finally had enough. Their chiefs held a secret meeting and decided to stage a surprise revolt.

The surprise was not complete. One of Ponce's men, an interpreter named Juan Gonzales, attended the meeting in Indian disguise and reported on what took place. But despite this warning the Tainos struck with surprising force. One Spanish settlement was destroyed and eighty of its inhabitants were killed. The *cacique*, Guaybaná, son of the friendly Aguebana who had once exchanged names with Ponce, killed the chief constable, Sotomayor, and all his men.

But then it was Ponce's turn. The Tainos did not have a chance. The furious Spaniards crushed them without mercy, and when the revolt was over, Guaybaná and two other *caciques* were dead and the *conquistadores* were more firmly in control than ever.

By now, Indian conditions—not only on San Juan, but all over the Spanish Indies—were so bad that many voices were calling for Spain herself to step in and try to ameliorate them. The loudest of these voices were missionaries of the Dominican order who had come to the Indies and were horrified at what they had seen.

Spain's answer to the outcries was the Code of Burgos, written in 1512 and meant to govern Indian relations throughout the western hemisphere.

This code was a compromise. Like so many compromises, it was not a very satisfactory one. It stated that the most important duty of both crown and colonists was to bring the Indians to a Christian and reasonable way of life. But despite the strong protests of the Dominicans, it held on to the system of *encomiendas* as the means to achieve this aim.

Although mainly defeated in the battle of the Code, however, the Dominicans were not ready to give up the war. They believed more and more that the Spaniards had absolutely no right in the New World. The land belonged to the Indians. There could be no moral justification for expropriating it or for forcing the Indians to labor.

The most famous—and probably the most unyielding—of the Dominican missionaries was Bartolomé de Las Casas, who was later (1544) to be appointed bishop of Chiapa in Guatemala.

Las Casas first came to the Indies in 1502 when he was sent to Hispaniola with Ovando. In 1512 he was ordained as a priest, and by 1514 he was in the forefront of those Spanish Dominicans who worked so hard for the Indian cause.

Las Casas traveled extensively throughout the Spanish Indies and fought for his beliefs in many places and in many different ways. In Spain itself he propagandized for new and stronger laws. When he felt that this was getting him nowhere, he tried to found a new kind of colony—one manned by decent Spanish peasants who were not afraid of doing their own hard work and who would, by their own examples, lead the Indians to a Christian way of life.

In 1520 Las Casas managed to organize a band of two hundred peasants who agreed to go to San Juan as members of an idealistic colony. They left Spain without the founding priest, however, and when they reached Puerto Rico they acted just as badly as did the colonizers who came before them.

Las Casas did not give up. The following year he actually settled seven men—two priests and five laymen—on the shores of what is now northern Venezuela. This was to be the beginning of a model community. While he was away trying to collect more pioneers, however—in what has to be called a tragic irony—Carib Indians set upon the small community and killed its seven members.

And still Las Casas did not lose faith in his Indian cause. He wrote and preached about it until the end of his days. Even when the hostility of his Guatemalan diocese forced the bishop back to Spain in 1547, he refused to compromise his beliefs and spent the final nineteen years of his life opposing Spanish colonial policy.

Perhaps the most vivid account ever written of the way the Indians suffered under Spain is in Las Casas' *Brief Account of the Destruction of the Indies*. Las Casas finished this paper in 1542, but it was not published for another ten years. In it, he placed the blame for the condition of the Indians squarely on the avarice of his fellow countrymen.

When the Indian rebellion of 1511 was crushed in San Juan, the troubles of Ponce de León were far from over. When Juan Cerón—the man whom Diego Columbus had appointed as governor of the island—arrived in Spain, King Ferdinand released him from arrest and sent him back to San Juan with a royal letter to confirm his position. This time Ponce had the bad news straight from his monarch. There was nothing for him to do but step down as gracefully as he could.

As a consolation, however, Ponce was given permission to lead another expedition, this time to the north. It was on this trip that he discovered Florida, which he believed to be an island.

In 1514 Ponce himself came back to Spain, bringing with him a large amount of gold smelted at the mint which he had constructed on San Juan. The king was pleased and delighted. Within another year Ponce was reappointed as governor of San Juan.

Upon returning to the island, one of Ponce's first moves was to divide it into a pair of districts, the larger of which he named Puerto Rico after the name he had first given the bay. He still had his problems with crown officials, however—problems that seemed to come to a head in 1519 when, over his strong objections, the capital of the island was moved from his own city of Caparra.

Although Ponce stubbornly remained in his fortified home in Caparra, the new city flourished. In 1521 the name of the new capital officially became San Juan Bautista, and the island as a whole was called Puerto Rico. In that same year, Ponce set out on his final expedition.

Ponce was wounded by Indians in Florida and sailed to the island of Cuba, where he died. In 1559, however, his remains were brought back to Puerto Rico. They were transferred to the Cathedral of San Juan (in the Old San Juan section of the city) in the year 1908.

Perhaps it was just as well that Ponce de León left Puerto Rico when he did. For changes were about to come to his island. And many of them were not good.

The Tainos—made weak by overwork, decimated by disease and Spanish bullets, driven to suicide by the utter hopelessness of their condition—were already fading from the scene. Within another seventy years, there would not be a single pure-blooded Indian left.

And the mines were giving out. No one could foresee it then, of course, and gold still poured out of the ground—but in the 1530's, production was to decline significantly, and by 1570 there would not be a profitable working mine on the island. The dream of Puerto Rico's golden future was to prove as unsubstantial as Ponce's own dream of the "fountain of youth" which he searched for and did not find in Florida.

The glorious first days of conquest and optimism were soon to be over on Puerto Rico. The island and its people would have to retrench. Indeed, there was to be real doubt as to whether it and they could survive.

THREE

DOWNHILL

But why this much of a decline? Puerto Rico, after all, was no barren wasteland. It was what it still is—a lush tropical island. Was there no other method but gold mining for the Spanish settlers there to support themselves?

One would think that there must have been. And the settlers tried to find it. One of their earliest efforts to reshape their economy was an attempt to replace gold with sugar as the island's number-one export.

At first glance, this must have appeared the ideal solution. The European demand for sugar was great and growing. The upper classes, who had to purchase this still scarce item in tiny amounts from apothecaries, were increasingly hungry for this fabulous sweet. If the island could help satisfy this demand, perhaps it would be able to weather the coming economic storms.

Spain agreed. Sugar could be an important commodity not only for Puerto Rico but for all of the Spanish Indies.

In 1529 the Spanish government showed just how deeply its colonial hopes were tied up in sugar. In that year a highly significant law was passed exempting sugar mill owners from having their property attached because of unpaid debts.

But despite government encouragement—and despite the fact that Puerto Rican soil and climatic conditions were just right for sugar growing—the production and refining of this product was not as simple as it might have seemed. It necessitated manpower, and lots of it. Land had to be cleared, sugar had to be planted, cane had to be cut, mills had to be constructed. Where were the men to do all of this? Who would supply the unskilled labor?

The first thought must have been the Indians. In their semi-feudal condition, it didn't matter what *they* thought of the idea. The Tainos would do what they were told.

But there weren't enough of them to go around. The Tainos were a dying race. As early as 1516, in fact, there had begun to be a shortage of labor in the gold mines. And by 1520 the Spanish crown had become so concerned with the Indian situation that it ordered local authorities to free all natives belonging to *non*residents (including those belonging to the crown itself) and to house those newly freed Indians in native villages. Furthermore, the order continued, all residents of the islands who did possess Indians should take steps to ensure that they would not be mistreated.

But this was an almost classic case of doing too little and doing it too late. It is possible that if the same order had been given ten or twenty years before, it might have done something to save the Taino population. Or it might not have. All we can say for certain is that, in the event, it did little to help.

And there was that increasing labor shortage that threatened to kill the Puerto Rican sugar industry before it could be properly born. What could be done about that? The best solution, the Spanish believed, was to import black slaves from Africa.

The first Negro slaves probably arrived in Puerto Rico with the first contingent of *conquistadores*. But slaves did not achieve great value until about the time when the Indian labor shortage was beginning to be felt. It was not until 1518 that the first mass shipment of five hundred blacks was introduced to the island.

Today, it may seem ironic that one of the strongest early proponents of the idea of bringing slaves to the Spanish Indies was Bartolomé de Las Casas. To the priest, however, it was a desperate measure designed to help save his Indians. It may be worthy of note, incidentally, that slavery was one of the very few of Las Casas' suggestions that the Spanish government wholeheartedly endorsed.

Beginning with that first shipment of 1518, slaves poured in—both to the Indies as a whole and to Puerto

Rico in particular. But there were never enough of them, and duty paid to the Spanish crown made them expensive.

In 1529, government representatives in San Juan urged that Negroes be imported duty-free. Naturally enough the request was not granted. Taxes paid by the slave traders were too profitable to the royal treasury at home. This entire situation was one that encouraged smuggling. And although island authorities cooperated with the Spanish fleet to try to put a stop to it, Puerto Rico's coastline was far too long and difficult to defend.

The Portuguese seem to have been especially adept at slave smuggling. And since smugglers do not pay taxes, they could afford to sell their human cargo at lower prices than the so-called legitimate slavers. When the island's money supply was low, as it usually was after the early years, the Portuguese were willing to be paid in barter.

It was not only the smugglers who were beating the duty system. Some licensed traders increased their legal earnings by importing more slaves than their licenses allowed for. In the year 1532, for example, it was estimated that licensed slavers brought in three times the number that they had actually paid taxes on.

While all this was happening, the island's economy was steadily going downhill. Hurricanes were scaring off shipping, raiding Caribs were harming both the crops and the population, and receipts from the sugar industry were lower than had been hoped for.

In 1544 a new blow hit the sugar industry—this one from the Spanish government. Instead of granting more incentives, as islanders were begging Spain to do, the government imposed a heavy new tax on sugar.

This tax was so onerous that many of the most important settlers were moved to protest it. One such protest came from Bishop Rodrigo Bastidas, who wrote to the king himself to explain the harmful effects that the tax must have on the industry.

The protests were apparently effective. Although high taxes continued, the crown began to lend settlers money in order to help them construct new sugar mills. All in all, however, Spain's shortsighted tax policy undercut the effect of these loans.

Apart from a brief flurry of hope in the early 1530's, when a few new deposits of gold were discovered, the mood of the people during this time was one of despondency. They must have felt betrayed. They had come to Puerto Rico to make their fortunes in gold, but now the mines were running dry. And sugar, which some had greeted as a substitute for gold, was proving not to be.

Then, in 1534, an event took place that made Puerto Rico's already nervous social situation even more unsettled. A ship sailed into the harbor bringing news of great gold discoveries in Peru.

Suddenly Peru became a magic word. Who could say what possibilities were there? Peru might turn out to truly be El Dorado—that mythical land of golden riches. Every Spanish settler on Puerto Rico seemed to have the same fervent prayer on his lips: "May God help me to go to Peru!"

The governor of the island, Francisco Manuel de Lando, was appalled. If his colonists all had their way, he would rule over an island depopulated of Spaniards. He ordered the ship to weigh anchor immediately, but the damage was already done. The settlers began to leave.

Lando fought the exodus by taking a whole series of repressive measures—even imposing the death penalty on any islander who tried to depart. But more and more Puerto Ricans were willing to take a desperate risk in order to gain riches. Some found boats in the small harbors on the island. Others made deals with the traders who were smuggling slaves into Puerto Rico.

For his part, Lando increased his watchfulness and repression. At one point, three of his ships intercepted an attempt to escape. When the party was captured, the governor had some of them flogged and ordered his men to cut the feet off others. Despite everything, though, still other Spaniards attempted to flee.

If the Spanish were unhappy, they at least had their dreams and schemes. There was no El Dorado for the Tainos. They were acting out the last days of their own tragedy.

The Spaniards were well aware of what was happening to the Indians. Many of them, both for humanitarian and for economic reasons, still hoped to do something about the situation.

In 1542 a last-ditch attempt was made by the Spanish crown. It hoped to save the native population in the Indies through a series of laws, called the New Laws, which were designed to eliminate the *encomienda* system once and for all.

The Indians were not slaves, the New Laws pointed out, but free people who were vassals of the king. Spain had always meant for the Indians to be treated in this manner, the document claimed. Now, the Council of the Indies—the governmental body responsible for the Indies—was instructed to enforce rigorously all the laws that were enacted for the protection of the Indians.

This time it appeared as if Spain meant business. Over and over again, the New Laws spelled out both the rights of the Indians and the obligation of the colonies to uphold those rights. Indians were not to be enslaved. They were not to be mistreated. Spaniards, the document stated—in what seems a surprising echo of Las Casas and the other Dominicans—had no authority at all over newly discovered Indians. Furthermore, in what was the most controversial ruling of all, the document held that no more Indians were to be given in *encomienda*. Indians currently in that state were to be freed—were to be handed back to the crown as free vassals, that is—upon the death of the current *encomendero*.

It was a brave try. But authorities today agree that the New Laws failed in their purpose. There was too much going against them. All over the Spanish Indies, wealthy and important settlers penned protests to Spain in which they darkly predicted the end of the Spanish empire if the new rules were enforced. Bowing to this pressure, the crown modified first one and then another clause.

When the smoke of controversy had cleared away, it could be seen that very little had changed. The *encomienda* system might have been shaken for a while, but it was still well entrenched.

On the island of Puerto Rico, certainly, the New Laws had practically no impact at all. Bishop Bastidas received the assignment of carrying them out. But he did not find many Indians left to liberate; eighty is the figure suggested by some reports. Despite the bishop's efforts and the efforts of the island's government, the few Tainos who were left alive in Puerto Rico were being secretly sold as slaves as late as 1550.

The Caribs, however, were still going strong. It may be

a sad commentary on human nature, but the fierce cannibals of Guadeloupe and other nearby islands lasted far
longer than did the gentle Tainos of Puerto Rico. The
Spanish could not seem to control the Caribs, and their
raids against Puerto Rico became bolder and bolder.

It was already mentioned that they raided the island's
capital in 1529. One year later they returned in even
greater strength and laid waste the countryside surrounding San Juan.

At that time (October 31, 1530) about five hundred
Caribs came in eleven war canoes. They landed at a spot
near the capital that was called Daguáo, and according
to an official report, they plundered the estate of Christopher Guzmán, the principal settler. The death toll included
Guzmán himself, several other Spaniards, and many Negroes and Indians. "They burned them all," the report
goes on to state, "and committed many cruelties with the
Christians. They carried off twenty-five Negroes and Indians, to eat them as is their wont."

The constant threat of Carib attack had the settlers
living in fear. According to one official, the women and
children of the capital no longer dared sleep in their own
homes for fear that the Caribs would sneak into the city
and burn them. They spent their nights in the stone church
or monastery while their men guarded the city and the
roads.

In their desperation, the settlers called for help. Spain's
response, however, was both poor and slow. In 1532 the
crown did send two small ships to help guard the coastline
and also authorized the building of new fortifications. But
the ships proved unfit for service, and the islanders were
forced to use the money meant for the fortifications to
construct two new boats.

With Spain hesitating to act, the Puerto Ricans decided
to depend on themselves and launched a series of attacks
on the Carib islands. In 1534 they fitted out an expedition
against Dominica, and in 1536 and 1539 they attacked
Carib strongholds on Trinidad and Bartolomé.

These strictly do-it-yourself expeditions had some success. But their cost to the already impoverished Puerto
Ricans was tremendous. The 1534 expedition alone cost
more than four thousand pesos to outfit.

The worst of it, however, was that the punitive attacks
were no real solution. They would hamper the Caribs

temporarily, but they were not strong enough to knock them out and destroy their potential for raiding.

As for Spain herself, she might have been able to do something if she had set her mind to it. But Puerto Rico was hardly worth it.

FOUR

UNDER SIEGE: *The French*

At this point a natural question comes up: If Puerto Rico was so poverty-stricken and the situation there seemed so hopeless—if Spain thought it hardly worthwhile to defend the island from Carib attack—why not give up on it altogether? From a purely practical point of view, might it not have been wiser simply to abandon Puerto Rico and call it a poor investment?

On the face of it, certainly, there would appear to have been some justification for such a decision. In the early days, gold from Puerto Rico added to the wealth of Spain and—not so incidentally—helped to make that nation one of the wealthiest and most powerful on the European continent. But that time had passed. Now the island was a drain on its mother country.

Despite all of this, however, Spain apparently never even considered pulling up stakes and getting out. Why?

One reason, of course, must have been Spanish pride. Puerto Rico *was* Spanish—one of Spain's overseas possessions and an exemplification of Spain's civilizing and Christianizing mission to the Western world. Cutting off Puerto Rico would have been like cutting off a part of herself.

But there was a far more practical reason for holding on to Puerto Rico. The island, as Governor Francisco Manuel de Lando wrote in 1543, was "the key and the entrance to all the Antilles." Unless Spain wished to endanger her entire role in the Indies—including those colonies which did produce great wealth for her—she could not afford to abandon Puerto Rico. The island was too strategically situated. With one shore facing the Caribbean and the other facing the Atlantic Ocean, it controlled the trade routes to Spain's possessions in the New World.

The very fact of Puerto Rico's central location and strategic importance, however, created more troubles for the settlers there. Other European powers had men who could read charts and figure strategy. And Europe could breed raiders who were at least as dangerous as the Carib Indians—even though they might not have the Caribs' cannibalistic habits.

The fact that it took some time before other European nations decided to threaten Spain's role in the Indies was partly due to a papal bull issued in 1493 by Pope Alexander VI. In it he attempted to prevent any future argument over the Indies by granting the rulers of Spain the exclusive right to trade and acquire territorial possessions one hundred leagues west of the Azores.

There was nothing unusual in what Pope Alexander attempted to do. As spiritual head of Europe, the pope claimed the right to adjudicate in matters of trade. He had already (in 1455) granted similar rights in southern Africa to Portuguese rulers.

The papal bull did help to keep the peace temporarily. But by the 1520's the lure of the West Indies' wealth proved too much for political morality or religious scruples to cope with. More and more Europeans were asking themselves the same sharp question that has been attributed to King Francis I of France: Where were the divine writings which granted half a world to Spain and Portugal?

King Francis, at least, apparently decided that those writings were not to be found. Starting with the year 1521, French privateers were active in the Indies and openly attacked Spanish shipping there.

A sixteenth-century privateer was a hard man to pin down. He was a cross between a pirate and a naval officer. As a pirate, he preyed on both merchant shipping and undefended towns, made a profit on anything he was able to capture, and paid his crew from that profit. As a naval officer he held a commission from his king—who could often be his patron, as well—and was expected to carry out his country's foreign policy.

When France turned loose her privateers against the Spanish Indies, therefore, these bold seamen were fulfilling two functions: They were furthering the designs of King Francis I and they were enriching themselves.

Like all European nations, France led a precarious existence, in which war was a common state of affairs. In the first five years of Francis I's reign—he ascended the throne in 1515 at the age of twenty—he had fought and won battles against the Italians and against the Swiss. But Francis still felt threatened, and a powerful Spain made him particularly nervous.

Then, in 1519, something happened which appeared to confirm his worst fears. Both he and Charles I of Spain were rivals for the position of Holy Roman emperor— actually the emperor of Germany and Austria. Charles was elected, becoming Emperor Charles V, and was crowned by the pope at Aachen. He now threatened France both from his original base in Spain and from his new position in Germany.

As a partial response to this changed situation, King Francis decided to strike out at Charles's vulnerable Spanish possessions in the Indies.

Soon a fleet of French privateers had stationed itself at a small island between Puerto Rico and Hispaniola. From there, the fleet kept a keen lookout for Spanish merchantmen.

Although the privateers happily ate up Spanish merchant shipping, however, there were no direct attacks on the island of Puerto Rico until 1528. In that year, two French ships made a hit-and-run raid on the western part of the island. Men from those ships looted and burned the small settlement of San Germán.

The Puerto Rican settlers found themselves becoming demoralized. Raids by the Caribs were bad enough. But now French pirates were attacking them, too. They pleaded with Spain, begging for some protection. In 1529 the construction of a fortress was authorized.

Work did not begin on the fort for another few years, however, and the structure was not completed until some time before 1540.

When the fort was finished, it was obviously not satisfactory. Its location was wrong. It would not protect the harbor and was easy for raiders to avoid by the simple expediency of sailing around it. Its placement so incensed one influential settler, González Fernández de Oviendo, that he condemned it as a piece of useless work which could not have been set in a worse place "even if it had been constructed by blind men!"

Oviendo suggested the placing of some cannon upon a rocky promontory known as El Morro (the cliff). From here, he pointed out, the entrance to the bay could be guarded. Needless to say, this advice was taken and the battery on El Morro gradually grew into Fort Morro—or Morro Castle—which is now San Juan's most famous landmark.

The original fortress has had an interesting history, also. It was badly damaged by the Dutch in 1625, rebuilt, and made into the governor's residence by 1640. Today, after several reconstructions, it is still being used as the executive mansion. Known as La Fortaleza, it claims to be the oldest executive mansion still in use in the western hemisphere.

The French privateers staged another raid in 1538, when San Juan's fort was almost complete. The French sailed prudently around it (they needn't have; it was desperately undergunned) and once more burned and sacked San Germán.

This time, however, the Puerto Ricans were more ready for them than they had been ten years before. The settlers came out in force, mounted a counterattack, and forced the privateers back to their ships.

But the privateers were not discouraged. They came back to the island again and again. They returned in 1540, in 1541, and in 1543. Each time, they would torment the coast, burn plantations, and—according to pattern—sack the town of San Germán.

Puerto Rico appeared helpless against them. La Fortaleza was not doing its job, and the entire island was short of artillery. It was not until 1555, when eight bronze cannon were placed in the new bastion on El Morro, that the ordnance problem began to be solved.

In the year 1544, though, international events once more took a hand in Puerto Rican affairs. This time they gave the battered island a respite, albeit a brief one. In a new treaty with Spain, King Francis I agreed to recognize Spanish rights in the Caribbean. French privateers, therefore, were no longer granted their all-inclusive hunting license in the Indies.

For a time, people even dared hope again. Perhaps Puerto Rico might now have a chance to develop its agricultural resources in order to attempt an economic comeback.

As long as France and Spain stayed at each other's throats, Spain had less interest than ever in spending her time and money to help Puerto Rico's development. What she did spend went into the war.

There were many in the colony who did not approve of this emphasis. In 1541, for example, at the height of Puerto Rico's first harassment by France, the island's treasurer, Juan Castellaños, wrote to Spain: "Forts for this island are well enough. But it would be better to favor the population, lending money or ceding the revenues for a few years to construct sugar mills. . . ."

The Spanish crown, however, was in no mood to take this advice. It apparently even resented the necessity of sending money to build defenses for such an out-of-the-way and unproductive spot as the island of Puerto Rico. After authorizing (in 1540) the construction of a fortress to guard the town of San Germán, it ordered the work halted two years later. Year after year, the residents of this town pleaded in vain for the Spanish crown to resume work on the fortress.

During this period the social discontent that broke into the open in 1534 with the discovery of Peruvian gold, grew still worse. The settlers, bitter at their lot, felt that crown officials were not responsive to their needs. Almost from the beginning, they had complained about the activities of many officials. Governor Lando's extreme measures to keep them from leaving were a final straw.

In 1537 the growing turmoil helped resolve Spain to try an experiment. From now on, the crown ordered, the island's ruling officials would not be appointed. They would be elected from among the colonists by a board of eight *regidores,* or aldermen.

This early flirtation with democracy was not a success. Since the governor was elected from among them, the settlers refused to take his decisions as final and managed to appeal almost every one. In 1542 one resident begged the crown to appoint a governor whom people would fear. "If someone of this class is not sent soon," he wrote, "he will find few to govern, for the majority intend to abandon the island."

The king resumed his old prerogatives in 1544, although Spain did continue to experiment with an elective system for Puerto Rico from time to time.

As far as Puerto Rico was concerned, the peace with France was never a complete one. Privateers continued to plunder the island on their own—even at the risk of their king's displeasure. But those occasional raids were nothing compared to what had been going on. In Puerto Rico's weakened condition, even an occasionally broken truce was better than no truce at all.

The island was to find that out for itself in 1552—the year the war was officially resumed. Then, in the following year, things got even worse. The infamous French privateer François le Clerc came into the Caribbean.

There did not seem to be any stopping Le Clerc, whom the Spaniards called *Pie de Palo*—Peg Leg. He sliced through the Indies like a knife, bringing death and destruction in his wake. He attacked and pillaged Puerto Rico, Cuba, Hispaniola, and many other places. For a time he brought Spanish shipping practically to a standstill and threatened to destroy the entire Spanish colonial system.

In 1554 the French made their most devastating attack yet on the town of San Germán. This time they completely demolished it. The townspeople had had it. They left the vulnerable location that had been selected in 1512, moved their village inland, and began all over again. The new town, San Germán el Nuevo, is standing today, although it too was attacked by the French—in 1569 and 1576.

So it went. The French came back time after time. For a while, the islanders must have spun dizzily under what seemed a never-ending series of attacks which they could neither avoid nor successfully defend against.

Actually, however, the Puerto Ricans soon would be able to defend their island from attack. Their means of defense was slowly taking shape: the great and growing monster of Fort Morro.

We have already seen that eight bronze cannon were placed on the cliff in 1555. By 1584 the castle grounds of San Felipe del Morro were laid out. Within ten more years the fort would prove its value as the guardian of the harbor. Fort Morro would continue to grow taller and thicker until 1776, when it finally reached the imposing size that it is today.

But all this lay in the future. In the meantime the raids of the French privateers were beginning to run down, almost as if of their own accord. The French still came, but less and less often. And the island was beginning to worry less about them.

This did not mean that the settlers' troubles were over. Far from it. For, if they were worrying less about France, it was at least partly because of their growing concern about another country whose ships were challenging Spanish ones for supremacy of the seas.

England was on the move.

FIVE

UNDER SIEGE:
The English and the Dutch

There is no space here to go into the complexity of causes for the long and drawn-out enmity between Spain and England. Part of the trouble was undoubtedly religious in nature. England, which had always had a certain amount of conflict with Rome, had been officially Protestant since the Reformation of 1532 under King Henry VIII, while Spain was the leading Catholic nation in Europe.

The prime cause of the difficulties between the two countries, however, had to do with commercial rivalry. In the new mercantile climate of the day, England could not exist as an insulated island sufficient unto itself. Forced out of its former possessions on the European continent, it had to expand its worldwide trade. And Spain, with its exclusive trading rights to so much of the New World, was an enormous obstacle in England's path.

For these and other reasons, England and Spain became sworn enemies in the second half of the sixteenth century.

Britain's interest in the Western world began shortly after Columbus' first voyages of discovery. As early as 1497, John Cabot, a Genoese who made his home in England during the reign of Henry VII, sailed across the Atlantic to North America. But although Cabot did travel far enough south on a later trip to approach Florida, he was apparently ordered not to poach too near Spanish territory.

For as long as relations between Britain and Spain remained good, indeed, the English were most careful to respect Spanish rights in the Indies. All official trade between England and the Spanish colonies was carried out through Spanish ports, from which goods from the Indies could be transshipped to England.

This is not to infer that there was no *clandestine* trade between individual English ships and the people of the Spanish isles. There was a great deal of it—and for the most natural of reasons: Both islanders and shipmasters were eager not to pay the Spanish crown taxes.

The first British ship to trade in this manner with Puerto Ricans was probably the *Mary Guildford*, which stopped at the island in 1527. It was a completely friendly call, with none of the bitter conflict that was to mark so many later meetings between Britons and Spaniards. The English crew traded with the islanders and then sailed off again.

During the next several decades, English ships continued to pay secret visits to Puerto Rico and the other Spanish possessions. These visits were not detailed in official reports, and the only way we know about them is through a general complaint by the Council of the Indies which was concerned about the loss of revenue to the Spanish crown.

At this same time, events in Europe once more conspired to cast a long shadow over the Caribbean.

Tension was building between Elizabethan England and the Spain of King Philip II. Queen Elizabeth was still doing her best to avoid an outright state of war with the wealthier and numerically superior Spanish, but she did decide to borrow a leaf from the French book and send privateers to harass Spain's West Indian colonies.

The man she placed in charge was Sir John Hawkins, a merchant captain and former slave runner from Plymouth who was later to design the English fleet that fought the famed Spanish Armada. Although Hawkins cruised throughout the Indies, he never landed on Puerto Rican soil. His elder brother, William, was there, however, in 1582 or 1583.

The Hawkins brothers taught their trade to other members of their family. Among them were John's son, Richard, and a kinsman named Francis Drake.

It was Drake who became the most hated and feared privateer of his day. The Spaniards used his name as a curse word and termed him "the master thief of the unknown world."

Drake made many voyages to the Indies both by himself and with his old mentor, Hawkins. As his fame spread in England, he became influential with the queen herself. By the early 1580's he was one of those men urging Elizabeth to bring Spain to her knees by completely throttling her trade with the West.

Another member of this same "war party" was Sir Richard Grenville. In 1585, in an attempt to prove just how defenseless the Spanish Antilles really were, Grenville led an expedition to Puerto Rico. His men disembarked and began to construct a wooden fort in defiance of the Spanish settlers.

When the Spaniards met the English under a flag of truce, Grenville coolly presented his list of demands. What the English wanted, he said, was food, water, and friendly treatment. If they did not get treated fairly, they would have to use force.

The Puerto Ricans agreed to everything and then departed. The British waited confidently for their return—until they slowly came to realize that the Spanish had no intention of returning. Perhaps unnerved by this experience, Grenville burned the fort and sailed away to hunt for Spanish merchantmen.

A little later, incidentally, Grenville was to accept remarkably lavish hospitality from the Spanish governor of Hispaniola.

In 1569 Queen Elizabeth decided to unleash Drake. She sent him to the Indies with orders to do his worst.

Although Drake stayed clear of Puerto Rico itself, the islanders were very much aware of the fact that he was raiding nearby islands. Church authorities were especially apprehensive about the effect that the Protestant English might have on their church and on their Indian converts.

The whole Caribbean breathed easier when Drake was pulled back, shortly thereafter, to guard the waters near England. A series of sea battles ensued, climaxed by the defeat of the Spanish Armada in 1588.

Now that Spanish sea power was reeling, many Englishmen wanted to carry the war to Spain itself. But England had neither the ships nor the men for an invasion. She had to return to her earlier tactic of harrying the Spanish merchant fleet. This, she hoped, would not only obstruct Spain from rebuilding her strength at sea, but also provide enough loot to pay for Britain's armed adventures.

Spain, perfectly aware of the British strategy, was determined not to be caught napping. All over the Indies, preparations for the war were being made.

In Puerto Rico, work on Fort Morro was intensified. The island's governor, Diego Menéndez de Valdés, was confident that his people would give a good account of themselves in any battle against the English.

Over the next few years, the English engaged in minor probing operations which tested the defenses of Puerto Rico and other Spanish possessions. The queen, however, was worried about leaving her own shores unprotected. She still hesitated to order the major blow against the Indies that many of her bolder subjects were urging.

In 1595 the queen finally made up her mind. Drake and Hawkins would lead an expedition to the Caribbean.

When the British fleet reached the Indies they received a piece of what was for them excellent news. The flagship of a large convoy—a ship that was carrying some two million pesos in gold—was damaged in a storm and had to put into San Juan for repairs. The gold was taken to Fort Morro for safekeeping.

Drake responded to this news like a bloodhound on a hot scent. Not even the death of Hawkins from disease on November 12 could dampen his spirit. Here was booty ripe for the taking. He would make a swift, surprise attack—a favorite Drake tactic—grab the gold, and be off!

But things were not to be so easy. For once, Drake was unable to spring one of his famous surprises. The Puerto Ricans had been expecting something like this for years. They knew their Drake; they knew what he would do. Then—some six months before Sir Francis actually showed up—Spain's intelligence service had warned Governor Menéndez to prepare himself for an attack by Drake.

The English fleet appeared on November 22 and exchanged shots with several Spanish frigates in San Juan Bay. Then the island's defenders brought the guns of Fort Morro into play, and the English ships had to beat a hasty retreat. When the British sailed back on the following day, they carefully stayed beyond the range of the Spanish land-based artillery.

That night, the night of November 23, Drake played what he thought would be his trump card. A group of about twenty-five launches were sent out in a surprise attack on the Spanish frigates. At first everything went the way the British expected—with the launches setting some of the frigates on fire.

But this proved to be a serious miscalculation on Drake's part. The light from the burning launches lit up the bay as bright as daylight, and the Puerto Rican shore batteries boomed out with murderous accuracy.

Drake made a few other futile attempts to breech the defenses, then withdrew in search of easier game.

No one could have blamed the Puerto Ricans if they celebrated long and hard after the English fleet departed. Fort Morro and the other Spanish defenses had withstood a crucial test. Sir Francis Drake, the scourge of the Indies, had been sent away with his tail between his legs.

But the English themselves were not so easily discouraged. Three years later, in 1598, George Clifford, the Earl of Cumberland, was to lead another and more successful raid against the island.

Cumberland did not attack Puerto Rico by accident. His major objective—though kept secret when he left England—was to succeed where Drake had failed and to capture this gateway to the Spanish Indies.

To ensure the success of his task, he led a fleet of eighteen ships, including his own flagship, the *Malice Scourge*. He also came with a carefully thought-out strategy. Instead of sailing boldly into the harbor—an act which would bring him, as it had Drake, under the guns of Fort Morro—he would land his men east of the capital on an undefended beach in what is now the Santurce section of modern San Juan.

Even though they were outnumbered and taken by surprise, the Puerto Rican defenders fought back as best they could, making an exceptionally gallant stand on a bridge leading into San Juan. But the Spaniards did not have a chance. In addition to all their other disadvantages, they had been severely weakened by a fierce epidemic of dysentery which had recently ravaged the island.

Mile by contested mile, Cumberland and his men forced their way through the capital. In the end, they forced the Spaniards to take refuge in their stronghold of Fort Morro. Then, after a siege of two weeks, that too fell to the British. Cumberland was master of the island.

In England, the news of the capture of Puerto Rico was received with tremendous excitement. For the moment, at least, it appeared as if Britain would permanently control this vital Caribbean outpost. Unknown to the people in England, however, nature was already rewriting their script. The great epidemic which had so weakened the Spanish was already striking at the English occupying troops.

Cumberland was now in a quandary. The ranks were being thinned by dysentery and yellow fever. All in all, some four hundred of Cumberland's men died from these diseases while many more were severely weakened by the ailments. Even so, he might well have hung on to the island if the population had been hospitable to him. But they were not. Stubbornly loyal to Spain, the Puerto Ricans harried and harassed the British whenever and wherever they had the chance. And although Cumberland was able to control the capital, the Puerto Rican countryside was in a constant state of rebellion.

Cumberland left Puerto Rico in August of 1598. He had been on that island for about three months. When he sailed away again, he had little to show for his stay there except the stores of hides, sugar, and ginger that he took back to England with him.

The British and the French were not the only races that contested Spain for the Indies. The Dutch, although starting later than the original three, were no less fierce— either in their desires or in their ability to fight for them.

During most of the sixteenth century, Spain controlled the Netherlands. By the end of that century, there developed a fierce and seemingly endless struggle for independence, a struggle with economic and religious overtones. And like the English, the Dutch used their privateers to threaten Spanish trade in the Caribbean.

It was not until the first part of the seventeenth century, however, that the Dutch threat became a dangerous one. In 1621 Holland organized its Dutch West India Company. Three years later the company landed men on the coast of Brazil, which—following the unification of Spain and Portugal—was under Spanish control. For a brief while, the Dutch even held Brazil's seventeenth-century capital city of Bahia.

In 1625 the Dutch decided to move on the island of

Puerto Rico. On September 25, sentries on Fort Morro spotted a Dutch fleet sailing into San Juan Bay.

The Puerto Ricans had been burned badly by the Earl of Cumberland. They had learned the lesson he'd taught them too well. They moved troops out of the city to prepare for a landing at Cumberland's old spot to the east.

But the Dutch commander, Boudewijn Hendrikszoon, had anticipated this reaction. He came into the harbor of San Juan and had his troops ashore almost before the Puerto Ricans realized what was happening.

This stroke paid off. Taken as much by surprise as they had been before, the Spanish soldiers were soon pushed back into Fort Morro.

This time, though, the Puerto Ricans were prepared for a siege. The island's governor, Juan de Haro, had made a bad mistake at the outset. But he was not going to make many more. He was determined to fight—and fight he would.

Twice, Hendrikszoon wrote letters to Haro demanding Puerto Rico's surrender. Each time, the governor turned him down. When the Dutch threatened to burn the town unless the Spaniards gave up, Haro replied that the settlers had "enough courage to rebuild their homes." He then advised Hendrikszoon not to write him any more such letters, as he had no intention of replying to them.

The exasperated Dutch carried out their threat. But it did not achieve the desired effect. For when the Puerto Ricans saw their capital in flames they staged a furious counterattack which threatened to bottle up the Dutch fleet in the harbor.

Baffled as well as angry now, the Dutch retreated to their ships. But even as they watched the invaders sail off, the Puerto Ricans realized how narrow was their victory. They could not feel safe, they knew, until they improved their defenses once again.

An essential part of this Dutch-inspired improvement was a great city wall which was started in 1631. The wall would take about 150 years to complete. When it was finished it would rise to as much as sixty feet above the level of the sea and entirely surround San Juan.

In connection with this wall, the Puerto Ricans planned a new fortress placed on a promontory about half a mile to the east of Fort Morro. This developed into Fort San Cristóbal, which was completed in 1778.

SIX

THE BUCCANEERS

By now, we have seen the Puerto Ricans suffer through and fight off raids by Carib Indians, by the French, by the English, and by the Dutch. But none of these raiders—as fearful as they were—could be called the worst enemies of the settlers. That distinction must be reserved for the grinding, day-to-day state of poverty in which most of them had to live.

Economically, the island was still caught in a quagmire. The only real industry was agriculture—and that was not doing well. We have already seen how sugar failed to help the economy. Ginger, which was Puerto Rico's other major crop, suffered repression at the hands of a government that felt it might interfere with the shaky sugar industry!

At the same time, memories of a golden past added to the problems of the present. Although there simply was no more gold on Puerto Rico, people still dreamed of finding new veins. How *could* such a fabulous producer be completely used up, they asked themselves. It did not seem possible. It was true, nonetheless. And the unrealistic dream of finding gold simply interfered with efforts to face the island's problems realistically.

But how could those problems be successfully faced and solved? At one time it seemed as if Spain must provide the answers. Puerto Rico was a Spanish colony; Spain would simply have to come through with subsidies and other forms of aid.

But the likelihood of this was dimming fast. By now,

Spain was well on her way to becoming, in our own overworked phrase, a "second-rate power." Unending warfare was ruining her. She never really recovered from the loss of her proud Armada. And other great Spanish fleets suffered the same fate. The latest—though certainly not the last—of a whole series of naval disasters was suffered in 1630 off the coast of Brazil at the hands of the Dutch. And Spain's military drain was not confined to the sea. The flower of her manhood was buried on battlefields all over Europe.

No nation could suffer this constant loss easily— certainly not while trying also to maintain a far-flung empire. Even if Spain had *wanted* to help her colonies (something which is in doubt), she was not able to do very much for them.

If Puerto Rico was to survive, therefore, she had to do so through her own resources—meager as those resources might seem.

One of the major obstacles to Puerto Rico's employing her resources to the utmost was Spain's restrictive trade policy.

Ever since Spain first founded her colonial empire, her colonies were permitted to do business only with and through the mother country. In every exchange of goods between a Spanish possession and another nation, Spain insisted on taking her cut: Spanish shipping had a monopoly on transportation to Spain, where Spanish merchants could make their profit and the Spanish crown could collect its taxes.

The other major European powers were not pleased by this state of affairs. Many of the attacks against Puerto Rico, for example, were at least partly brought on by reaction to Spain's restrictive trade policies. And the fact that the early attacks had all turned out poorly from the raiders' point of view did not mean that England, France, and the Netherlands wouldn't keep trying to change the Spanish attitude by one means or another.

In 1662, to take one instance, the governor of the (by then) British island of Jamaica was instructed to obtain a trading agreement with Puerto Rico—by negotiation if possible; by force if necessary.

When the Spaniards firmly turned down the British negotiators, the stage might well have been set for a new invasion. But after a closer look at Puerto Rico's newly strengthened defenses, the English made up their minds that force would not be such a good idea after all, and concentrated their attentions on Cuba instead.

The French and the Dutch also made overtures to Spain concerning a direct Puerto Rican trade agreement. They had no better success than did the English, however.

Thus the official Spanish attitude remained unchanged. But the Puerto Rican settlers had other ideas. Although extremely loyal to Spain in time of war, they suffered far more from the mother country's trade policies than did those who wished to trade with them. With willing sellers and eager buyers, therefore, smuggling became almost inevitable.

The first smugglers to reach the island came during the 1520's with the growth of the Puerto Rican slave market. The new rise of smuggling a century later was also associated with slavery.

This time it was the Dutch—operating from the island of Curaçao, which they had occupied in 1634—who were supplying Puerto Rico with illegal slaves.

Nor did the Dutch confine themselves to smuggling in human cargo. They would bring in many other articles that the settlers wanted and needed, taking out Puerto Rican cattle and foodstuffs in return.

The English and the French were only a short distance behind the Dutch in getting into the smuggling business with Puerto Rico. The English operated out of their own slave-trade center of Jamaica, and the French smugglers visited Puerto Rico from Tortuga and St. Christopher.

Even while the Puerto Ricans were trading with smugglers and freebooters from the island possessions of non-Spanish powers, however, they lived in dread fear of the unfriendly return of those same men. The same Dutch or English buccaneer whom they had just bought from or sold to might well come back to raid their coastal towns or capture their fishing vessels.

The fears of the islanders were far from empty. Spanish merchant ships had long been considered the "legitimate" prey of the buccaneers. But they did not mind bagging some smaller game as well. In 1644 a high Puerto Rican church official wrote that island fishermen were so afraid of capture that they did not dare to venture beyond the confines of the harbor.

Despite the fact that Spain's empire and her power

were rapidly starting to shrink, both she and her Caribbean possessions fought back as best they could. But Spanish expeditions against the pirate bases were usually inconclusive.

In 1640, for instance, Puerto Rico mounted an expedition to clear Dutch buccaneers from the island of Santa Cruz. When the engagement was over, the pirates were in disarray. Many of them were killed; others were taken prisoner. Hardly had the Puerto Rican forces left, however, before a new contingent of freebooters had occupied the island.

A similar situation developed ten years later when the Puerto Rican governor ordered an attack on the pirate base on San Martín.

In 1673, with a new outbreak of war between Spain and France, the entire buccaneer problem took on a more ominous note. Not only was the French government giving official backing to the privateers once more, but it appeared as if Puerto Rico was again to be the object of a massive invasion.

In 1678 one of France's most successful naval commanders, the Count d'Estrées, was apparently under orders to destroy both Puerto Rico and the Dutch island of Curaçao. This threat was dangerous enough to worry the British, who, although they would not have minded seeing the status quo changed, did not want it changed in just that direction.

Fortunately for the Puerto Ricans, nature—in the form of the sea—decided to take a hand. The French fleet tackled Curaçao first and ended up smashed on the rocks off the nearby Isle of Aves.

It was at about this time that a fifth power entered the Caribbean: the Danes.

Historically, Scandinavians had had a long association with the New World. Vikings from different sections of Scandinavia pushed past Iceland to Greenland and beyond Greenland to explore the North American shore. These adventurers might well have been the very first Europeans to set foot in the western hemisphere.

But Viking contacts with the West were confined to the far north and were ended some time before Columbus made his own southerly crossing. It was not until 1672 that the Danes came to St. Thomas to join the Spanish, the French, the English, and the Dutch in Caribbean waters.

St. Thomas lies in the Virgin Islands—quite close, in other words, to Puerto Rico. And Danish privateers there posed a definite threat to the island. But if that weren't bad enough, the Danes began to cast their eyes on a still closer point of land, the tiny, deserted island of Vieques—only eighteen miles from the Puerto Rico shore.

The Spaniards were not the only ones who were concerned about Danish nationals taking over Vieques. The British, ever jealous of their Jamaican slave trade, had no use for a new set of rivals in such a strategic position. They laid claim to ownership of Vieques and, in 1685, decided to found a colony there.

The English colony was placed under the command of a Captain Pellet, who—whatever other qualities he had—was not a very good soldier. When the Spaniards sent the fleet that they were bound to send and the inevitable bombardment began, the good captain lay down behind a barricade and tightly shut his eyes. Following the leadership of its military commander, the colony quickly surrendered and left the island deserted again.

In the meantime, Denmark decided that it too might as well claim legal ownership of Vieques. And in 1699, when a Scottish trading company attempted once more to hoist a British flag over the island, the Danes showed up with their own flag. After thinking it over, however, both countries decided to back away from Vieques before it became a three-way fight with the Spanish.

Until now, Puerto Rico's role in connection with the buccaneers was that of either victim or customer or both. They purchased smuggled goods from the pirates and privateers who, in turn, raided their island and captured their boats. But they were about to play a different part.

In the last quarter of the seventeenth century, Spain began to issue her own letters of marque. She herself was going into the privateering business.

This was great news for a number of people. Spanish sailors were delighted. They would at last be able to take revenge for the humiliation of so many of their countrymen. Now it would be their turn to chase *British* merchantmen around the Indies.

It was good news for Puerto Rico, too. As the Spaniards became more adept at privateering, they needed a friendly port in which they could deposit their prizes and repair any damage done to their ships. The island of Puerto Rico was an obvious choice.

The islanders welcomed these new visitors with open arms. And why not? The very sight of them must have given a great boost to the sagging Puerto Rican morale. These were not mere pirates, after all, not mere freebooting buccaneers. They were officially commissioned by the crown of Spain. By welcoming them, the Puerto Ricans were not only having their revenge on the much hated British but doing their patriotic duty.

And there were more practical reasons to make the Spanish privateers feel welcome and happy. They were bringing new wealth and new employment to the island. Puerto Rico, therefore, found privateering a profitable new industry—and one on which her economy would more and more come to depend. In a real sense, then, Puerto Rico *was* helping itself by means of its own resources: its strategic location, its harbors, and the willing spirit of its people.

Nor would the Puerto Ricans be satisfied for very long to play a merely passive role in the business of buccaneering. Before very long a growing number of islanders would be sailing out to privateer for themselves.

SEVEN

THE BRITISH KEEP TRYING

For her part, England was less than enchanted with the Spaniards' decision to switch roles from that of victim to that of victimizer.

As long as the game was played by British rules, everything had gone along smoothly. British, Dutch, French, and Danish privateers would capture Spanish merchant ships and raid Spanish possessions. Spain and the island governments would do their best to retaliate with punitive expeditions. The privateers and the northern powers would all make some money while the Spanish fleet got some exercise. There was a certain amount of rivalry between the buccaneering powers, but on the whole it seemed like a sensible arrangement.

But now Spain was throwing away the script. Everything was topsy-turvy. The Spanish—and even the Spanish colonials—were attacking British shipping. This could cost England money.

It did. Puerto Rican privateers, such as the feared mulatto captain, Miguel Henríquez, were anathema to the British merchant fleet. They sailed the Caribbean as though they owned the sea, and the English found themselves in the unenviable position that the Spanish themselves had occupied since early in the sixteenth century.

Puerto Rico helped provide a legal cover for the activities of her *guardacostas*, as the native privateers called themselves. The Spanish crown issued a commission to the Puerto Ricans which permitted them to protect their island by picking up foreign ships on suspicion of piracy and taking them into their home port. Crown officials at the port would then decide if the foreigner was actually guilty.

In Puerto Rico, at least, it was a rare vessel which the officials did not condemn. Any British merchantman sailing near the island (and because of its location, that included just about every British ship bound to or from the Indies) was likely to be herded into San Juan harbor and convicted of piracy. Her cargo was confiscated and sold, with the privateers and the government sharing in the profit and the local crown authorities taking their personal cuts. As for the merchant captain and his crew—they were most likely to wind up in jail.

In 1727, with a new outbreak of war between England and Spain, the Spanish and Puerto Rican privateers grew more active than ever. And at the same time, England once more turned her eyes toward Puerto Rico.

To the English the island must have seemed even more valuable now than it might have been before. Not only did it keep all its former attributes, but it was also a protected sanctuary of the *guardacostas*.

A detailed plan was drawn up by which the British thought they could take the island with some two thousand troops plus naval support. But a peace which was declared in 1729 called a halt to the plan before it could be implemented.

If peace reduced the activities of the Spanish and Puerto Rican privateers, however, it certainly did not put a stop to them. Miguel Henríquez and his colleagues carried on much as they had before—and again with the probable tacit approval of the Spanish crown.

Smuggling also continued, even though it was practiced now more with the French, the Danes, and the Dutch than with the English, whom most Puerto Ricans considered to be rivals and perpetual enemies. Nowadays, indeed, smuggling had grown so profitable that more and more crown officials were being corrupted by it.

One of the most powerful of these officials was Governor Matías de Abadía, who may well have been the prototype for hundreds of corrupt officials of Spanish colonialism who were to be later portrayed in fiction and drama. Once Abadía obtained his exalted position in 1731, he set about achieving a near monopoly on the island as a receiver of smuggled goods. In his heyday, he controlled five stores which also had a near monopoly as provisioners of ships.

The Spanish crown, which had no idea of Abadía's less respectable activities, applauded the governor's diligence in keeping out British smugglers. To him, this was just good business. They were not only enemies of Spain, but his commercial enemies as well.

In 1739 an English shipmaster named Robert Jenkins claimed not only that his ship was boarded by Spanish privateers, but that they cut off his ear as well. This story, which may well have been true, incensed British public opinion and the off-again, on-again war was on again.

The so-called War of Jenkins' Ear found Admiral Edward Vernon already in the Antilles in charge of a large fleet which captured Porto Bello, on the present-day Panamanian coast and laid siege to Cartagena, on the coast of what is now the Republic of Colombia.

The Puerto Ricans were understandably nervous concerning Vernon's intentions toward them. The British fleet sailed to Cuba, however, and tried to attack that island. After failing there, Vernon led his ships into more southerly waters and finally passed around the Horn into the Pacific.

On the island of Puerto Rico, in the meantime, Governor Abadía was in his glory: The Spanish crown had given him the rank of brigadier. He oversaw the strengthening of Puerto Rican defenses, encouraged the *guardacostas,* and prepared himself for any emergency.

When a peace of sorts had broken out again, little had changed on Puerto Rico. Smuggling, however, had grown even more pronounced. Now even the English smugglers paid bolder and bolder calls on the island.

By 1761 King Charles III of Spain was concerned enough by what he knew was happening on the island to send an emissary, Marshal Alejandro O'Reylly.

O'Reylly was an Irishman who worked in the service of Spain. One of the things he did on coming to Puerto Rico was to take a census of the island. He found that it held a total population of 44,883, including 5,037 slaves. This population, O'Reylly reported to his king, was basically loyal to the crown.

O'Reylly also told King Charles that the smuggling situation, though often harmful to Spain in other areas, was quite useful in Puerto Rico. It helped build up the island's economy, he said, and increased Puerto Rican productivity.

As far as helping the island was concerned, O'Reilly had several concrete suggestions. He advised—as had so many others—that Puerto Rico's sugar industry should be aided, and thought that the crown should quickly finance a new mill. New trade laws were urgently needed, he reported, and new economic measures had to be taken.

As a military man himself, O'Reylly was very concerned with building up Puerto Rico's armed forces. He felt that the army suffered from lack of discipline, while the island's general winking at graft had infected military officers. To combat this, O'Reylly instituted a number of wide-ranging reforms which greatly increased military efficiency.

Puerto Rico did not need to call upon its newly efficient army for another thirty-five years. Two more wars between Spain and England (1761-1763 and 1778-1783) came and went before Puerto Rican soil was again involved. But then, in the war which began in 1796, the island had to undergo one of the most severe tests it had ever faced.

Now, as had happened in the past, Spain was allied with France against her traditional British enemy. This time, England was determined to solve the nagging problem of Puerto Rico once and for all. There was going to be no more nonsense with the *guardacostas* sailing from there. England would take over their island, thus depriving them of their sanctuary and adding their fertile island to her own overseas empire.

Preparations for the attack were carefully made. Rear Admiral Henry Harvey was given a command of some sixty ships, while the six to seven thousand troops on board were placed under Lieutenant General Sir Ralph Abercromby. Their orders were specific enough. They would go first to Trinidad, and assuming things went well there, they would head for Puerto Rico.

Things did go well. Abercromby and his men landed on Trinidad in February of 1797 and took the island with ease. The fleet reached San Juan by April 17.

But San Juan was a far different nut to crack. By now, its city walls stood tall and imposingly thick and its defenses were literally bristling with cannon. It's true that the island was short of troops—only about two hundred regulars were there—but Governor Don Ramón de Castro had mobilized four thousand militiamen plus every other able-bodied male he could find.

After the usual formalities, in which Abercromby demanded the city's surrender and Castro politely refused, the British decided to imitate the Earl of Cumberland's old trick. They attempted a quick push from the east. But Abercromby was not as fortunate as the earl had been. The British were met by a furious artillery barrage and a no less furious resistance from the native militia.

For the next thirteen days there were skirmishes, attacks, and counterattacks. Abercromby could see that he was getting nowhere. Some of his own troops were beginning to desert, and there was little more he could do to force the issue.

Later he was to admit that the Spaniards were very well prepared and to claim that they had more troops than he had. "The troops, indeed, were of the worst composition," he wrote rather bitterly, "but behind walls, they could not fail to do their duty."

Another military man who visited Puerto Rico some thirty-five years later, however, took a somewhat different viewpoint. Colonel John D. Flinter—who, like Marshal O'Reylly, was an Irishman who served Spain—thought that Abercromby was foolish to have attempted to take the town.

"Sir Ralph's object in landing," Flinter wrote in 1832, "surely, could only have been to try whether he could surprise or intimidate the scanty garrison by which it was defended. However, from what I have been able to learn on this subject, it appears, that had he not re-embarked very soon, he would have had to repent his temerity; for the shipping could not safely remain at anchor where there was no harbor, and where a dangerous coast threatened their destruction. His communication with the country was cut off by the armed peasantry who rose *en masse*. . . ."

For whatever the reason, Abercromby did decide that he'd had enough. He returned to his landing beach and loaded his men aboard the waiting ships. When the Spaniards came out to attempt a counterattack on the morning of May 1, they found that the English had gone.

That was the last serious invasion of Puerto Rico until the United States came to the island in 1898—more than one hundred years later.

During the coming century there would be several minor raids by Colombian revolutionaries, who, incidentally, received short shrift from the Puerto Rican population. But no major power, during that time, would attempt to capture and control the island for itself.

Puerto Rico could rest easily for a while. Her defenses were strong; her people were loyal.

EIGHT

CONTACTS TO THE NORTH

Until 1776 and the War for American Independence, the United States of America, of course, did not exist. What was to become the United States consisted then of a group of thirteen colonies which were under British rule as Puerto Rico was under the rule of Spain.

Starting with the first half of the eighteenth century, several of the original colonies carried on a clandestine trade with Puerto Rico. By 1766—ten years, that is, before the American Revolution—ships based in Philadelphia were calling at San Juan on an almost regular basis.

When the North American colonies revolted against Britain, Spain was faced with a decision. As a European monarchy with an empire of her own, she could not really approve of a revolution against any crown. But on the other hand, she did not approve of England either.

The Spanish dislike for England won out. The king of Spain issued orders which permitted American privateers to put into the ports of his West Indian possessions in emergency situations.

The following year such a situation arose. Two United States barks, running away from a heavily armed British man-of-war, headed into the port of Mayagüez, which is located in the western section of Puerto Rico. The English frigate sailed in after them, demanding to be allowed to capture the rebel "pirates."

The Spaniards of Puerto Rico thought fast—then hoisted their own flag over the two American vessels.

The English captain protested furiously. He knew very well that the barks were not Spanish. But his protests fell on deaf ears. The Puerto Ricans held firm, and since England and Spain did not happen to be at war at the moment, that ended it.

Once the Revolutionary War was won, the United States asked Spain for permission to trade legally—on a limited scale—with Puerto Rico and other Spanish possessions in the Caribbean. The Spanish—nervous about continued smuggling and afraid that merchants in the United States could undersell those in Spain—refused to grant the request. Giving the enemy of Spain's enemy a helping hand was apparently one thing. Trade, even limited trade, was something else.

By 1790 Spain was forced to change her mind. Her own wars had by then crippled her merchant fleet. And she needed large stocks of food and other items to resupply her naval ships that were fighting in the Indies. The most convenient place to purchase whatever she needed was the United States. Trade with the States therefore began again—and on a legal basis.

In 1795, for example, Spain purchased huge amounts of American flour and other foodstuffs which were sent to Puerto Rico in order to provision a war fleet which was scheduled to stop there. The fleet did not arrive on time, however, and the food was still stored in San Juan when the British arrived to lay siege to the city. One reason that Governor de Castro was able to defeat Abercromby, in fact, was that he had this large supply of American food available to feed his militia.

A couple of years after that purchase—in November of 1797—Spain decided to completely open Puerto Rico and other of her island possessions to trade with the United States. At this point, naturally, the volume of trade grew enormously. The island was able to ship its products openly and directly to the north, receiving food, gunpowder, and other items in exchange.

But this situation could not last long. Business interests in Spain itself were severely hurt by the new set of rules, and lobbied vehemently to have the rules abolished. Furthermore, the French also wanted to keep American interests out of the Caribbean, and since they were allied with the Spanish at that time, they were able to exert a good deal of pressure to this end. The upshot of all this was

that the new trade laws were revoked in 1799. Spain's
West Indian empire was banned from carrying out any
direct trade with the United States—except under special
permits.

But this resumption of restrictions was destined to be
almost as short-lived as the freer trading policy had been.
In 1804—with Spain once more at war with England—
many Puerto Rican harbors were opened up to all neutral
shipping, including ships of the United States.

After this, trading contacts between the two countries
continued to grow. And the traffic flowed both ways. In
1807, for instance, eighteen Puerto Rican ships visited
Philadelphia. In two more years, that number had increased to thirty.

That this trade was good for the island cannot be
doubted. However, like Puerto Rican trade generally, it
was a negative one. Since its earliest days, Puerto Rico's
imports had greatly exceeded its exports.

No community can exist forever with a negative trade
balance. Puerto Rico would have gone into bankruptcy
long before if it had not been continually subsidized to the
amount of 500,000 pesos a year from the royal treasury of
Mexico.

Spain had enforced the *Situados Mejicanos*, as the sub-
sidy was called, since the first part of the seventeenth
century. It was this money that, among other things, paid
for the maintenance of the island's military defenses.

In 1811, however, as part of Mexico's movement toward
independence, the *Situados* came to an abrupt halt.

When this happened, the island of Puerto Rico was
plunged into a financial panic. The money from Mexico
had been supporting them for so long that the islanders
had begun to look upon it almost as a natural event, like
the regular arrival of the rainy season or like the fish that
swam in the Caribbean. They had never thought about its
stopping one day. Now that it had, the people literally
did not know what to do.

The small amount of money left in the Puerto Rican
treasury quickly gave out. The government tried to refill
its coffers by commandeering church funds and judicial
deposits. It sent out a call for private loans. But this
money was also used up. By 1812 there was no place left
to hide.

In desperation, Governor Meléndez began printing paper money which—because of lack of public confidence—

was soon proved almost worthless. A bad inflation followed and Puerto Rican poverty, which had been a serious matter since the 1530's, grew even worse. Some solution *had* to be found. And soon.

The solution was to set up an island Treasury Department—or *Intendencia*—and place a good man in charge: The brilliant civil servant Alejandro Ramírez, who had formerly served in Guatemala, was to be the first *Intendente* of Puerto Rico. He would have the job of trying to clean up the island's economic mess.

Ramírez took over his post in 1813 and wasted little time in getting to work. He immediately organized a public lottery in order to raise new funds and started to replace the inflated paper money with *macuquinas*—crude silver coins originally brought to the island from Venezuela.

Even more important than these emergency measures, however, were Ramírez' long-run accomplishments in the field of trade. The *intendente* understood that his only hope of making some lasting improvement in Puerto Rico's economic situation was to improve the balance of trade and that his best hope of doing that was to encourage freer trade with the United States.

In a proclamation issued on April 1, 1815, Ramírez reduced the duty on a number of different items, including flour and other foodstuffs, soap, machinery, and furniture. He also stated that every assistance and protection would be given to United States merchants trading in Puerto Rico.

In response to these actions, the United States government took the step of sending a commercial agent to San Juan. This agent, John Warner, served on the island from November 27, 1815, to April 9, 1818. He was the first official American representative in Puerto Rico.

The *intendente's* policies clearly worked. As legal trade replaced illegal smuggling, the trade balance grew more equal. Reasonable taxes took the place of the humiliating *Situados Mejicanos* as a means of paying for government functions.

To see the real difference that these policies made, one has only to note that in 1813 the income from legal trade equaled $269,008, while by 1816 the total had risen to $1,082,299. Just two years after that improvement, in 1818, the total had risen still further to $2,103,498.

As the years passed, more and more of Puerto Rico's trade was carried on with the United States. By 1830 more than 27 per cent of the island's imports came from the United States, while she shipped some 49 per cent of her exports to the northern republic. In that same year, it is worthwhile to note, 213 United States ships entered the different ports of the island.

Concerning this subject, Colonel John D. Flinter wrote in 1832: "The trade which is carried on between the United States and Puerto Rico is more advantageous to the latter than that of any other nation."

It is a well-known fact that trade breeds other contacts. And led by their mutual interests, contacts between the United States and Puerto Rico grew closer. Just where those contacts were to eventually lead, of course, no one could have guessed.

NINE

A MEASURE OF FREEDOM

The nineteenth century, both in Europe and in the Western world, opened to the thunder of revolution. The American and French Revolutions, which were the two most portentous of these, occurred within the last quarter of the eighteenth century. But the shadows they cast were long ones, influencing events all through the nineteenth century and, indeed, down to the present day.

In the year 1808 the warrior-child of the French Revolution, Napoleon Bonaparte, marched into Spain. He threw the newly crowned king, Ferdinand VII, into prison and placed his own brother, Joseph Bonaparte, on the Spanish throne. The loyalist people of Spain joined with the British and Portuguese to help push back the French in what became known as the Peninsular War (1808-1814).

As the fortunes of war favored first one side and then the other, repressions by the French against the loyalists became more severe, and many of the more influential patriots took refuge in the southern seaport city of Cádiz, where a strong movement toward liberal reform was already in progress. Here the *Cortes*—or Spanish parliament—which had been a mere rubber stamp for the crown, was reestablished and a constitutional monarchy was planned.

Spain's colonies reacted in different ways to the troubles of their mother country. Many of them revolted. Mexico's struggle for independence began in 1808, shortly after the

French invasion of Spain. Venezuela's independence came soon after Mexico's. By the middle of the 1820's, only the islands of Cuba, Puerto Rico, and the Philippines were left under Spanish control.

In the face of this almost frighteningly swift disintegration of Spain's far-flung empire, Puerto Rico stood firmly loyal. Though—as always—severely strapped for cash, the island made a large financial contribution to the Spanish cause. In 1808, with the war against France spreading to the Caribbean, Puerto Rico sent a contingent of men and weapons to aid in forcing French invaders from the island of Santo Domingo.

The reward for this loyalty was to be representation. In Cádiz the liberal-leaning *Cortes* ruled that from now on, Spain's colonies were to be considered a part of Spain herself. As such, they would be invited to send their own representatives to the *Cortes*.

The invitation reached Puerto Rico in 1809. The man chosen as the island's delegate was Captain Don Ramón Power y Giralt, a native-born Puerto Rican who had been educated in Spain. Power had already shown his loyalty to the mother country by being the naval commander in the successful fight against the French on Santo Domingo. He appeared to be an ideal choice.

Power quickly proved to be not only a distinguished naval officer with a fine family background, but a good diplomat with a flair for political in-fighting. Shortly after the *Cortes* opened, he brought honor to himself and to Puerto Rico by being elected vice-president of that Spanish organization.

But Power had not been sent to Spain merely to win honors—however welcome those honors were. He was instructed to work for a freer trade policy and more self-rule for the island. Together with other delegates from the Spanish colonies, Power struggled hard to effect these changes.

He was amazingly successful. One of his first accomplishments was to convince the *Cortes* to limit the authority of the crown-appointed governor of Puerto Rico, who—because of Spain's constant fear of revolution—had been granted the right to detain on his own orders any person he considered to be a threat to public safety.

Having won the battle against this and other of the governor's dictatorial powers, the delegate turned to the subject of free trade and the Puerto Rican economy. Here too he was successful. Spain set up an independent Puerto Rican *Intendencia* and placed Alejandro Ramírez at its head. We have already seen what followed as a result of this move.

By now it must have seemed as though Puerto Rico was at last assured a large measure of freedom and self-government. But this was not to be.

In 1814 Napoleon abandoned Spain and released the imprisoned king. Ferdinand VII reentered the country, promising to uphold the liberal constitution of 1812. His own preference, however, was for a return to authoritarian and despotic rule, and when he reached Spain, he quickly realized that the great mass of the people, the army, and the church were on his side. Taking advantage of the temper of the times, he chose to ignore his promise. He suspended the 1812 constitution and ignored the *Cortes*.

On the island of Puerto Rico, the return to tyranny was greeted with resentment. But where other colonies continued to rebel, Puerto Rico did not. The only thing that could even be called a Puerto Rican protest movement was the one led by Rafael Diego and Demetrio O'Daly. But this apparently dwindled away without having much effect.

By the middle of 1814, the island's first period of comparative political freedom was definitely over.

At this time—despite the improvements made by Power and Ramírez—the twin forces of poverty and ignorance were still rampant in Puerto Rico.

While the wealthier classes could afford to send their young men to be educated in Spain, education for the common people was practically nonexistent. In one of its few educational gestures, in fact, the island government offered to *sell* spelling books to anyone wishing to learn how to read.

But however rough it was for the ordinary citizen, the class which suffered most horribly from Puerto Rican poverty was the slaves. Left practically without any legal protection, they were forced to share in their island's trials and tribulations, while not being permitted to share in its few triumphs.

The British, who were now working to abolish the practice of slavery in their own empire, offered to pay Spain an indemnity to halt the slave trade in hers. The offer was accepted in 1817. Spain agreed to stop her slave traffic by May 30, 1820, in return for an amount equal to $20 million, which was to be used to compensate those Spanish subjects who had been engaged in it.

But once he got the money, King Ferdinand had other plans for its use. He bought a fleet of thirteen warships from Russia and forgot all about his deal to abolish the slave traffic. Slaves were not emancipated in Puerto Rico until March 22, 1873.

As time went on, slave revolts on other islands—such as on Haiti, where the revolt culminated in a black republic—left the Puerto Rican slave owners frightened. They could not help asking what would happen if such a revolt took place on their own island and the *free* Negro population joined together with the slaves.

From their point of view, that could have been a dangerous situation. In 1830, for example, whites on Puerto Rico outnumbered the slaves by 162,311. But in that same year there were 127,287 free blacks. Numerically, in other words, the two groups were roughly equal.

In 1843, therefore, the then governor-general, John Prim, gave vent to the general feeling of white insecurity by issuing a number of Draconian decrees designed to control *all* Negroes, whether slave or free. Among these rules was one that stated that "any individual of African race, whether free or slave, who shall offer armed resistance to a white, shall be shot, if a slave, and have his right hand cut off by the public executioner if a free man."

For minor offenses, according to another decree, slave owners were permitted to punish their slaves without interference from any government official. And, if a slave should rebel against his master, the master was authorized to kill him on the spot.

But to return to the more fortunate—although far from ideal—life of the white citizens of Puerto Rico: In 1820 a new Spanish upheaval restored the constitution of 1812. Once more, these Spanish events had their effect on Puerto Rico. The island was again considered to be an integral part of Spain and was invited to send another representative to the newly restrengthened *Cortes*.

The man chosen now was Demetrio O'Daly—the same O'Daly who had done his best to fight against the return of despotism in 1814. It was largely through his efforts that a number of improvements took place on the island, including a separation of military and civilian authority.

This second period of freedom lasted until 1823. During that time the Puerto Rican press, which had been tightly muzzled by censorship, was given an extraordinary degree of liberty, while local politicians were permitted to harangue the populace on just about any subject, including the formerly taboo one of island independence.

Perhaps the surprising thing is that the Puerto Ricans did not seek to revolt from Spain then, when the bars were lowered and they had a chance. But unlike so many Spanish colonials, the people of Puerto Rico by and large preferred to remain loyal to their mother country.

In 1823 the roof fell in again. French troops marched into Spain to restore the king who had been held prisoner by the *Cortes*. On regaining his throne, Ferdinand refused to honor his promise of amnesty, and a new wave of repression began, both in Spain and in Spanish possessions overseas.

Conditions in Puerto Rico became even worse than they had been after 1814. Firmly in control again, Ferdinand VII was determined to have no more nonsense about island representation. The press was muzzled again, politicians were ordered to stop agitating, and those men who were identified too closely with the reform cause either were tossed into jail or had to flee into exile.

One of the exiles was Demetrio O'Daly. The former delegate to the *Cortes* lived for a time in London and then went to St. Thomas, where he earned his living as a language teacher.

One surprisingly good result did come out of all this. The Spanish crown named a new governor of Puerto Rico, Miguel de la Torre, who used his dictatorial powers not simply for repression, but to bring about real economic change.

La Torre cleaned up much of the organized corruption that remained on the island and increased public revenues to the extent that the army and the civil service could expect to be paid regularly and in full for the first time. Until La Torre took over, the island was continually in arrears in paying its employees.

La Torre also encouraged trade and embarked on a necessary program of public works. According to John D. Flinter, "more was accomplished for the island during the

last seven years of Governor la Torre's administration, and
more money arising from its revenues was expended on
works of public utility, than the total amounts furnished
for the same object during the preceding three hundred
years."

During the final years of his life, King Ferdinand's
fading health caused him to place more and more power
in the hands of his queen, María Cristina. She, while
hardly a liberal reformer, was at least somewhat less
despotic than her royal husband.

One piece of Puerto Rican evidence to this is that in
1832 an island Supreme Court was inaugurated in San
Juan. This meant that the administration of justice could
now take place entirely within Puerto Rico. Until the new
court was set up, legal cases in Puerto Rico could be
appealed to the *Real Audiencia*, which was located first in
Santo Domingo and then in Cuba.

In the same year a seminary was founded in the Puerto
Rican capital to enable young men to receive a secondary
education.

King Ferdinand VII died a year later, in 1833, and a
series of civil conflicts erupted over the succession of his
daughter, Isabella II, and her mother, María Cristina,
who reigned for ten years as regent.

In Spain this period was marked by despotism which
alternated with short periods of comparative reform. In
Puerto Rico there was very little reform.

In 1837 the island was placed under military rule. Captains-general came over from Spain—a total of twenty-six
of them between 1837 and 1874 alone—to control the people with a firm hand and to keep a sharp eye out for any
possible show of rebellion.

The very first of these military gentlemen set the pattern
for most of the others. When Don Angel Acosta came to
the island in 1837, he did so with the avowed purpose of
stopping any revolutionary tendency dead in its tracks. His
methods included repression on the one hand and "circuses" on the other.

Acosta's idea of "circuses" was gambling. He built cock-
fighting pits in almost every town on the island, on the
theory that as long as people "dance and gamble they
don't conspire."

The theory might well have had something to it—for
many other governors followed suit. By 1865, gambling

was endemic on the island and it was estimated that there was a gambling house on almost every street in San Juan. When protests were made concerning one notorious gambling house that was seriously fleecing the Puerto Rican citizenry, Governor Felix Messina answered coolly. "Let them gamble," he said. "While they are at it they will not occupy themselves with politics, and if they are ruined it is for the benefit of others."

If these examples point to a certain contempt by the military governors for the people they controlled, that seems to be expressing the situation mildly. They believed firmly that Puerto Ricans were low forms of life who had to be ruled strongly and with—as one governor put it—the three "B's": *baile, baraja, y botella*—dancing, cards, and drinking.

That this official attitude would bring on resentment among the people is almost too obvious to need stating. Under the circumstances, few Puerto Ricans had any confidence or hope in the future. With poverty once more stalking the land, it would seem as though conditions were ripe for that very rebellion which the governors were trying to stave off by repressive means.

Conditions were very ripe. The more severe these measures became, the more people talked revolt—which, in turn, brought on more oppression. A climax of sorts came when a seditious movement took hold of the island's military garrison. Governor José María Marchessi not only bore down hard on the malcontents, but used the incident as an excuse to banish about a dozen of San Juan's leading citizens. Spain was later to disapprove of this action. But in the meantime it made for even more tension on the island. The grumbling not only grew louder, but more and more powerful people were doing it.

Then, in September of 1868, Queen Isabella II was deposed as queen of Spain and a temporary republic was set up by a triumvirate of military officers.

At about the same time, as if by telepathic osmosis, a revolution would be getting under way in Puerto Rico. This Puerto Rican revolution would have its comic-opera aspects. But its implications would be grave.

TEN

TWO PATHS

On September 20, 1868, two or three hundred Puerto Ricans of all races and backgrounds met together at a coffee plantation near the small mountain town of Lares, located in the western section of the island, about half-way between the northern and southern coasts. The purpose of the meeting? Revolution. The Lares rebels wished to end Puerto Rico's ties with Spain once and for all and set up their own republic, to be called Borinquen after the old Taino name for the island.

The rebellion was primarily inspired by two Puerto Rican exiles whom Governor José María Marchessi had banished for sedition: Don Segundo Ruiz Belvis, a former delegate to the *Cortes* in Spain, and Dr. Ramón E. Betances. Ruiz Belvis died while trying to obtain help for his plan in the former Spanish colonies which had already achieved their independence, leaving Betances to carry on by himself.

While both Ruiz Belvis and Betances were distinguished and formidable men, however, some of their associates were less than effective.

After picking up a supply of knives and machetes from the owner of the coffee plantation (a United States citizen named Bruckman), the revolutionaries marched to a second plantation belonging to a Mr. Rosas, who promptly introduced himself as their general-in-chief. Rosas was wearing an American fireman's uniform that was further brightened by a tricolor scarf and a flaming sash. In further token of his rank, he had on cavalry boots and carried a sword and revolver.

After a full meal, the revolutionaries made their way to the town of Lares itself. Some time around midnight, the sleeping citizens of that community were startled awake by cries of *"Down with Spain!" "Death to the Spaniards!" "Long life to independent Puerto Rico!"*

Town officials found themselves locked up along with any Spaniards still loyal to their mother country.

Despite the fact that they only controlled one small town, the independent Republic of Borinquen was declared the following day. A new government was set up, and Spaniards were given three days either to leave the island or to swear allegiance to the republic.

The rebels next marched to the nearby town of Pepino. There, in the town plaza, they fought a pitched battle with the town militiamen. A brief exchange of gunfire left the rebel group with one of its members dead and two or three wounded. At this point, the rebels, believing that the regular army had come, fled the scene. Rosas and a few of his faithful officers were left to face the enemy alone.

After realizing that there was no chance of rallying his troops for another stand, Rosas made his way sadly back to his own plantation.

So far, the effect of the revolt was minimal. And if the government had continued to ignore the rebels, there is little doubt that the event might well have been disregarded by the majority of Puerto Ricans.

But the government chose not to ignore it. As soon as he heard about the revolt, Governor Marchessi made up his mind to punish the revolutionaries.

He moved swiftly. Bruckman and one other man were killed, while the others were arrested and placed in detention under such unsanitary conditions that no less than seventy-nine of them died in an epidemic. Of those who managed to survive prison, seven more were executed.

This *was* shocking. And what followed was inevitable. Where hardly anyone bothered to take the Lares rebels very seriously before, they were now turned into martyrs and heroes.

In the meantime, Ramón Betances—who with his friend, Ruiz Belvis, had helped inspire the rebellion in the first place—had become an exiled symbol of Puerto Rican resistance to Spain. After the failure of the Lares rebellion, he spent time in Curaçao, St. Thomas, Venezuela, Haiti, and finally went to France, where he lived until his death in 1898.

Betances was one of the principal founders of the dream of a confederation of Antillean states, including Cuba and Puerto Rico—those two Spanish islands whose hopes for freedom were coupled together in many minds until the cataclysmic event of the Spanish American War.

Betances was not the only distinguished Puerto Rican who felt that freedom for his island could only come with complete independence and that this independence was inexorably bound up with independence for Cuba. Eugenio María de Hostos, for example, the great Puerto Rican crusader for better education, was to become a leader-in-exile of the Cuban Revolution and work on its behalf in New York. Betances himself was the official delegate in Paris of the Cuban Revolutionary Party.

Puerto Ricans were not the only ones to worry about events on their island at this time. Many Spaniards were also becoming nervous. Spain's empire was almost gone now. Was she about to lose those bits and pieces she had left? Perhaps it would be wiser for her to loosen the reins somewhat on Puerto Rico.

In 1869 all Spaniards (those who were still alive, at least) who had any connection with the Lares rebellion had their sentences commuted. And in that same year Puerto Rico was invited to send eleven deputies to the *Cortes*.

These new deputies, who included in their number Juan Hernández Arbizu and Luis Padiel y Vizcarrondo, fought hard for greater liberty in Puerto Rico. And in 1870 General Gabriel Baldritch Palan, a man of firm liberal beliefs, was sent to the island as governor.

Baldritch did his best to dispel the clouds of bitterness and distrust which hung heavy over Puerto Rico. He encouraged freedom of the press, built schools for secondary education, and gave islanders the right to elect their own town councils. Baldritch also set up a local elected assembly, known as the *Diputación Provincial*, which had its first meeting on April 1, 1871.

A good many of the Puerto Ricans themselves, however, were anti-reformist, and a violent opposition to these changes developed—especially among the wealthier classes. Frightened by the continuing revolutionary conditions

on Cuba, they did not hesitate to accuse the governor of
being an enemy of Spain who used his office to protect
local separatists. The feelings against him ran so high that,
on July 26, 1871, he was forced to declare a state of siege
in San Juan.

In September of that year, the anti-reformers got their
wish. Baldritch resigned in disgust. His replacement was a
man named Ramón Gomez, whose sobriquet, *coco seco*—
or dried coconut—tells something of his nature. He soon
was filling the island's jails with reformers.

In 1873 King Amadeo of Spain abdicated his office after
a reign of about two and a half years, and that tortured
country became a republic. One of the new government's
first acts was to order the abolition of slavery.

This was something that a good many of the more
enlightened Puerto Ricans had been fighting for. One of
the most eloquent voices in the Puerto Rican anti-slavery
movement belonged to José Julián Acosta, an island
statesman and scholar who was one of the many imprisoned after the Lares rebellion. In 1867 Acosta was in
Spain, where, in the company of other like-minded men,
he demanded complete and immediate abolition of slavery—with or without compensation to the slave owners.
Later, both as a delegate to the Spanish *Cortes* and at
home on the island, he repeated his plea of immediate
freedom for *everybody*.

The Spanish abolitionists won their point in 1873. The
Puerto Rican government was ordered to issue bonds in
the amount of 35 million pesos in order to indemnify the
slave owners. Puerto Rico's 29,229 slaves were at last set
free, and the date that the order was signed—March
22—was to be celebrated on the island as Puerto Rican
Abolition Day.

But if the islanders thought that Spain's change of
government would bring them any other social improvements, they were doomed to disappointment. Just the
reverse happened: Their popular governor, Primo de Rivera, was replaced with a hard-liner, José Laureano Sanz,
and under him, the clock was to be turned sharply back.
Schools were closed, the elected assemblies were dissolved,
and press censorship was reestablished. Life under a Spanish republic, the people soon learned, could be every bit
as despotic as it could be under the Spanish crown.

As a matter of fact, when the brief republican age was over and a new king assumed the throne of Spain in January, 1875, he at least made a gesture of restoring the town councils and the *Diputación Provincial* to Puerto Rico.

But King Alfonso XII's gesture was *only* a gesture. Discontent grew on the island—still partly nurtured by the revolutionary turmoil on the island of Cuba. The different governors tried to put down this discontent by the old policy of clamping down hard on anyone who might possibly be considered anti-Spanish, and this policy still did not work.

An additional factor was now adding to the collapse of island moral: The end of slavery had helped bring the economy once more to the point of ruin.

Having lost their cheap labor supply, the former slave owners did not have the cash to replace it with paid labor. Their indemnity was handed to them in the form of ten-year bonds—which they were later forced to sell at about 15 per cent of face value.

In 1887, with Spain steadfastly refusing to grant Puerto Rico the same concessions she had made to Cuba ten years earlier, a protest meeting was held in Ponce, Puerto Rico's second largest city, which is located some seventy-six miles southwest of San Juan, on the southern coast of the island. The assembly was under the leadership of Román Baldorioty de Castro, who, along with Acosta, had been one of the chief fighters against slavery in the Spanish *Cortes* of 1870.

Baldorioty was not a revolutionary. He did not want complete separation from Spain. He felt that there was another path to island self-government. He dreamed of an autonomous Puerto Rico—but one which still stayed within the Spanish system. Spain would still exercise sovereignty, but the island would control its own internal affairs.

It was during the Ponce convention that the Puerto Rican Autonomist Party was formed with Baldorioty at its head.

One of the newer stars at this convention was a thirty-two-year-old patriot named Luis Muñoz Rivera. Three years later he was to start the newspaper *La Democracia* in Ponce (it was later to move to San Juan), and in 1891 he was to assume leadership of the Autonomist Party.

Although autonomy was, in essence, a pragmatic move-

1. Ponce de Léon

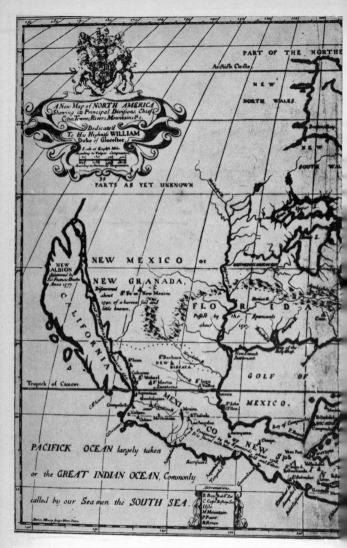

The following text appears within the map image:

PART OF THE NORTHE[RN]

Arctick Circle

NEW
NORTH WALES

NEW

SOUTH WAL[ES]

A New Map of NORTH AMERICA
Shewing its Principal Divisions, Chief
Cities, Townes, Rivers, Mountains &c.

Dedicated
To His Highness WILLIAM
Duke of Glocester.

Scale of English Miles
according to Vulgar Computation

PARTS AS YET UNKNOWN

Upper L[ake]

NEW
ALBION
discovered by
Sr Francis Drake
Anno 1577

NEW MEXICO or

NEW GRANADA,

C
A
L
I
F
O
R
N
I
A

Discovered
about
1592, a barren soil
little known.

Ste Fe or New Mexico

FL
O
R
I
D
A

Possest by the Spaniards
about 1527

New French
Settlement

S. Barbara

NEW
BISCAYA

GOLF OF

Tropick of Cancer

S. Thom

Culiacan
S. Michael
S. Martin
Zacatecas

Compostella
Guadalajara

MEXI

Mexico
S. Tabesta

Leon Argados

S. Lucar
S. Vallodi

S. Lin
S. Vluas

MEXICO.

CO
or
NEW
SPA

Conquered by the Spaniards
by Fra. Ferd with the Spaniards

PACIFICK   OCEAN largely taken

or the GREAT INDIAN OCEAN, Commonly

called by our Sea men the SOUTH SEA.

Pacifica

Abbreviations.
B Bay, Bank of Sea
C Cape, B Bay, Sea
I Isle
M Mountain
P Point
R River

2. The earliest authentic map of Puerto Rico

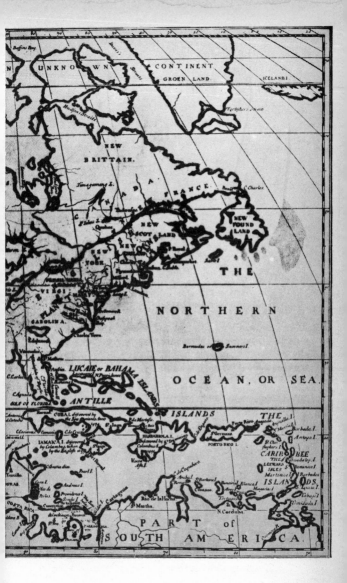

3. The ancient sea wall which protected San Juan from sea attacks. The sentry post in the background is part of La Fortaleza, the governor's mansion.

Puerto Rico Economic Development Administration

4. An artist's rendition of the sinking of the *U.S.S. Maine* in Havana harbor, February 15, 1898.

The Bettmann Archive

. Rexford Tugwell (left), the newly appointed governor of Puerto
Rico, being welcomed by his predecessor, Guy J. Swope (right), as
Luis Muñoz Marín, then president of Puerto Rico's Senate, looks
on, August, 1941.

Wide World Photos

6. Under the Land
Authority Program,
farm workers draw
lots for *parcelas,* small
plots of land upon
which they can erect
their homes.

Black Star

7. El Morro, San Juan,
Puerto Rico.

*Puerto Rico Economic
Development Administration*

8. Cutting sugar cane in Aguadilla, Puerto Rico.

Black Star

9. Former governor of Puerto Rico, Luis Muñoz Marín.

Wide World Photos

10. The impoverished community of La Perla, outside the walls of Old San Juan.

Black Star

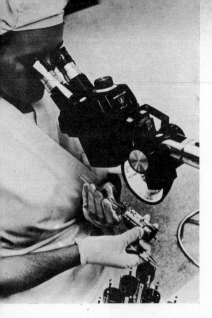

11. The electronics and electrical industry is made up mostly of branches of American firms. Over 80 per cent of the plants are affiliated to mainland companies.

12. An aviation mechanics operation at a Puerto Rican vocational school. There are many technical high schools in Puerto Rico.

13. Luis A. Ferré, former governor of Puerto Rico.

Puerto Rico Economic Development Administration

14. San Juan—the old and the new.

Puerto Rico Economic Development Administration

ment toward compromise, Spain was as fearful of it as she was of the complete revolutionaries. Her new representative on the island, Governor Romualdo Palacios, immediately began to repress all the leaders of the Ponce convention of 1887. Torture was used to gain information, and Baldorioty, Muñoz Rivera, and other Autonomist leaders were placed under arrest.

The reign of terror was so vicious that the governor feared that Spain itself would not approve of his tactics. He placed a strict censorship on outgoing communications and would not let word of what was happening leave the island.

Eventually, some Autonomists managed to escape to St. Thomas, from where they sent word to Madrid and brought the terror to an end.

In 1895 the two paths toward island self-government seemed to diverge still more. The leading Autonomist, Muñoz Rivera, visited Spain in order to come to some understanding with one of the Spanish political parties. In the same year, renewed revolutionary activity in Cuba convinced the Puerto Rican revolutionists that it was time to combine with the Cubans.

A Puerto Rican Section of the Cuban Revolutionary Party was established at a convention held in New York City, and Dr. José J. Henna, a physician who was born in Ponce, was elected president of this section. Ramón Betances, who once helped inspire the Lares rebellion, was made delegate general of the section in Paris.

The argument between those who believed in autonomy and those who believed that Puerto Rico could only gain her freedom through complete independence from Spain was a basic one. Though often buried, it was never completely laid to rest. In altered form, indeed—with the United States taking the place of Spain—it still continues today and is at the root of much Puerto Rican dissension and unrest.

Muñoz' first mission to Spain was a failure. But in 1896 he was able to come to an understanding with the Liberal Party of Spain, which was under the leadership of Práxedes M. Sagasta. By 1897 the agreement was formalized. When and if Sagasta's party came to power, Puerto Rico would be granted autonomy.

In the meantime the Revolutionary Party was making

plans for a revolt in Puerto Rico. General Juan Ruis Rivera, a Puerto Rican veteran of the earlier Cuban revolt, came to the island in order to study conditions. He found the people apathetic, however, and returned to Cuba.

In 1897 Sagasta's Liberal Party came to power in Spain. The leader kept his word. From now on, Puerto Rico would largely govern itself. The Spanish government would still appoint the governor general and would uphold its military rights and its sovereignty. But the island would be governed through an elected Chamber of Representatives and a fifteen-member Council of Administration, seven of whose members would be chosen by the governor and eight elected by the people.

It was a good plan, a workable plan. But it had come too late. Already there were ominous rumblings from the north. A new force was about to enter the scene.

ELEVEN

THE UNITED STATES INTERVENES

With revolutionary ferment coming to a head in Cuba, a war between Spain and the United States became all but inevitable.

To understand why this should have been—why what happened in Cuba did affect United States-Spanish relations—we must first digress for a bit of historical background.

Cuba's revolt against Spain was waged in two major stages. The first of these—the so-called Ten Years' War, which ended in 1878—was halted by compromise and Spain's promise of sweeping reforms. Spain, however, soon began to renege on that promise. In 1895 the Spaniards suspended constitutional guarantees in Cuba, and the already simmering kettle came to a boil again.

The war in Cuba began in the east, but it quickly spread throughout the island. It was a war that would be fought to the death, with neither side asking or giving quarter. Spain built a series of primitive concentration camps and filled them with Cuban civilians, who were forced to exist under the most barbarous conditions. The Cuban rebels retaliated with a scorched-earth policy on the ground that Spain would never give up their country until it was rendered completely worthless.

In 1897, when the Liberal Party leader, Práxedes M. Sagasta, came to power in Spain, he attempted to solve the Cuban problem in the same way he was solving the Puerto Rican one: by the promise of autonomy.

But too much had happened for the Cuban rebels to be satisfied with what they considered half a loaf. They did not want a Spanish-appointed governor with whom—in any sort of a crunch—final authority would have to rest. They would not take the path that Puerto Rico seemed to be choosing. They would hold out for complete independence from Spain. Sagasta's offer was emphatically turned down.

Although at first not wishing to do so, the United States found itself becoming more and more involved with the Cuban situation. America had been carrying on a $100 million trade with that Caribbean island. American business interests had made actual investments in Cuba which totaled some $50 million. All of this was now endangered. Wartime conditions had brought trade to a virtual standstill, while the scorched-earth policy of the rebels resulted in the destruction of U.S. investments in plantations, sugar mills, and other property.

Both President William McKinley, who took office in 1897, and his predecessor, Grover Cleveland, tried to keep the nation out of the conflict. But most segments of American society were beginning to believe that they had a common cause with the rebels.

America's western drive had about run its course by now. In its concern for new markets—its expansionist movement to achieve its "Manifest Destiny"—the United States was looking southward. Cuba, less than one hundred miles from American soil, and the strategically valuable island of Puerto Rico were within a "natural" United States sphere of influence. To Americans, Spain seemed like an intruder.

Add to this the American public's normal sympathy for the underdog, a feeling which was being whipped to a frenzy by the popular press. It is certainly an oversimplification to state that the Spanish American War was *caused* by a Hearst or a Pulitzer. But press competition was such that the papers latched onto all stories of Spanish atrocities as a means of raising their circulations, and thus undeniably helped prepare the American people to go to war with Spain.

Representatives of the Cuban rebels in the United States had an obvious interest in helping to whip up anti-Spanish feeling. So too did those Puerto Ricans, such as Dr. Henna, who believed that their island should also revolt against Spain.

The reverse was true of the Puerto Rican Autonomists. Far from welcoming a United States intervention, Muñoz Rivera, for example, insisted that the Puerto Rican people were Spaniards and would remain loyal to Spain. Puerto Ricans, he was to insist, would die wrapped in the Spanish flag.

In 1897, in the face of this propaganda war, President McKinley offered to mediate between the two sides. The Spaniards hedged on their acceptance, however. They were willing to accept some of McKinley's terms, but gave him what was, to American eyes at least, an unacceptable time limit for the reestablishment of peace.

Then, in December of that year, new riots in the city of Havana led McKinley to send a battleship into the harbor in order to protect American lives and property. The battleship, of course, was the *Maine*.

On the night of February 15, 1898, while riding at anchor, the *Maine* was struck by a giant explosion which sent her to the bottom along with the bodies of more than 260 of her crew.

No one has been able to fix final responsibility for the blast, which apparently resulted from a mine which, in turn, set off the vessel's forward magazine. But—whether the Spaniards, the rebels, or even some third party actually did the deed—the reaction of the American press was both loud and predictable: Spain had to be held accountable.

The New York Journal offered a fifty-thousand-dollar reward for "the Conviction of the Criminals Who Sent 258 American Sailors to Their Death." And just in case any of its readers hadn't guessed who those criminals were, another *Journal* headline shrieked: "NAVAL OFFICERS THINK THE MAINE WAS DESTROYED BY A SPANISH MINE."

Though still officially neutral, President McKinley had little room left in which to maneuver. Practically every American was repeating the popular slogan "Remember the *Maine*! To hell with Spain!"

Spain was only too aware of the mood of the United States. She also knew that she would have little chance of winning what would have to be a naval war against America. She tried desperately to negotiate, even offering to submit the question of Spanish responsibility for the sinking of the *Maine* to arbitration. But though notes were written, back and forth, it was all to no avail.

On April 20, 1898, the U.S. Congress declared that "the people of Cuba are, and of right ought to be, free and independent." The legislative body demanded that Spain immediately give up all claim to that island and authorized the President to enforce that demand by military means.

Within four more days, war had been declared.

By now, the Puerto Rican revolutionists were demanding, in stronger and stronger terms, that the United States free their homeland too from Spanish control.

It would make little sense, they argued, to free Cuba while leaving Puerto Rico to Spain. A Spanish Puerto Rico could always pose a future threat to Cuba, and perhaps even to the United States itself. America, they reasoned, should first save Puerto Rico from Spain, and then allow the Puerto Rican people to decide whether they preferred independence or annexation by the United States.

The Spanish American War turned out to be both brief and one-sided. Fighting began in the Pacific, on May 1. Commodore George Dewey destroyed the Spanish naval squadron in Manila Bay and permitted an American military force to enter the capital city of the Philippines. By August 13, Manila was in United States hands.

In Cuba the war went just as successfully from the U.S. standpoint. By the middle of July the Spanish fleet stationed in the waters off that island was put out of commission and the important city of Santiago was under American control.

In Puerto Rico, meanwhile, the Autonomist government was working at full steam to obtain whatever gains they could from Spain. Muñoz Rivera—who still did not wish the island to break with the mother country—was working on a program of important economic reforms.

Spain herself was frightened. She could see that Cuba and the Philippines were as good as lost. She did not want to lose Puerto Rico, the last of her important overseas possessions. On July 18, with both her Caribbean and her Pacific fleets destroyed, she asked France to intercede in achieving an armistice.

But Washington did not wish an armistice yet. Puerto Rico, the U.S. government was beginning to believe, was

too valuable to be permitted to remain in Spanish hands.
A final decision to invade the island was taken on July
24—just a few days after Muñoz Rivera published his reform program in San Juan, and exactly two days before
France officially communicated Spain's plea for peace.

On July 25 an American fleet approached the southern
coast of Puerto Rico. By July 6 the invasion was on.

How did the Puerto Ricans feel about the American
take-over? It is always hard to generalize about an entire
people, but a number of facts appear to be clear enough.

The entire war on the island lasted less than one month,
and almost everywhere the Americans went they were
greeted with flowers and hurrahs. Most of the common
citizens appeared to believe that the conquering army was
bringing a Golden Age in its wake, and that eternal peace,
liberty, and prosperity would follow the American flag. If
there were any doubters on the island—as there probably
were among the members of the Autonomist Party, for
example—they kept a discreet silence.

The initial enthusiasm was to undergo a very quick
shift, however, as U.S. intentions became evident.

An armistice was proclaimed on the island on August
17, 1898, and the formal announcement of the ceding of
the island to the United States was made by the Spanish
governor-general, Manuel Macías, on September 29.

As event quickly followed event, it was becoming clear
that Puerto Rico was not going to be independent as the
Revolutionary Party had wished. Washington considered
the island too small and too poor to be able to handle
independence. Nor was it going to keep the 1897 constitution which the Autonomist Party had worked out so
painstakingly with Spain. It was a permanent possession of
the United States by now, and the United States would
decide what was best for it.

Nor would the new American colony qualify for protection under the U.S. Constitution. It was too Spanish—too
"non-American"—to achieve statehood; too torn apart
and disrupted by war for even a small measure of self-
government.

As the Puerto Ricans saw so much of what they had
struggled for go down the drain, it is easy to understand
why so many of them looked longingly back to a romanti-
cized image of Spain. The Golden Age, instead of being
just around the corner, now seemed to have been in the

past, with a Spanish tradition, the Spanish language, and the Spanish culture.

One Puerto Rican intellectual, Cayetano Coll y Toste, in a speech made some ten years after the U.S. invasion, appears to have expressed much of the general disillusionment which had come to the island. As quoted by Edward J. Berbusse in his book *The United States in Puerto Rico, 1898–1900,* Coll y Toste concluded: "Our autonomous constitution is abolished and the Puerto Rican people changed—in fact, but without right—into a political orphan that is at the mercy of the American Congress."

TWELVE

MILITARY GOVERNMENT

After the trauma of invasion, as we have seen, came a period of hopeful waiting to see what the "Colossus of the North" was going to do.

Although this hopeful period did not last very long, the end did not come abruptly or happen everywhere at once. It took about two or three years for the mood of hostility to permeate most of the island.

In 1899 the manifesto of a newly formed political party could state with confidence that the then-current condition of Puerto Rico was to be merely a temporary one. Soon the island was to be given the status of a territory, and soon after that it was to be a full-fledged state.

It would have taken a bold prophet, indeed, to make such a statement after another few years.

On July 28, 1898, shortly after the United States invasion of the island, the general in charge of American forces issued a proclamation in which he promised the Puerto Rican people the greatest degree of liberty consistent with military rule. "We have not come to make war upon the people of a country that for centuries has been oppressed," Major General Nelson A. Miles said, "but, on the contrary, to bring protection, not only to yourselves but to your property, to promote your prosperity, and to bestow upon you the immunities and blessings of the liberal institutions of our government."

Brave words. It is even possible that General Miles

believed them. Yet only a short while later, he was to insist to a fellow general that the power of the United States military was absolute and supreme in Puerto Rico. The established island court system and municipal laws could continue to function, Miles said, but *only* for as long as they served the purposes of the occupiers, who had the right to change any of these around at any time. Furthermore—and this would prove to be of prime importance in shaping the future feelings of the Puerto Ricans toward the Americans—U.S. military personnel would not be subject to Puerto Rican criminal proceedings.

All of this does not appear to back up the general's statement about bestowing on the Puerto Ricans "the immunities and blessings" of liberal institutions.

On the other hand, the military occupation was not designed to give the Army *carte blanche* to loot, rape, or murder with impunity. Certainly not. Nor was it meant to permit military commanders to run personal fiefdoms in any manner they saw fit. U.S. officers and their men were expected to be guided by a high sense of duty and "traditional" American justice.

This did, however, indicate something about how the Americans felt about the Puerto Ricans. The islanders needed guidance. They were too poor, too ignorant, perhaps even too "foreign" to look after themselves.

On October 18, 1898, the Spanish flag was lowered over San Juan for the last time, and the Stars and Stripes took its place. According to a book on the island published in 1940 and sponsored by the Puerto Rican Department of Education, "many Spanish residents would have followed their troops to Spain had their departure been made easy."

As it was, their departure was made extremely difficult if not impossible. The main problem was the one of converting their property and possessions on the island into cash under the new conditions of occupation. Some of the more intensely loyalist of the Spanish population took their losses and returned to Spain anyway. Others waited nervously with the rest of the islanders.

One of the things they were all waiting to find out was what sort of man the new military governor, Major General John R. Brooke, would turn out to be. It was Brooke who took over from General Miles on October 18, 1898, in order to head a peacetime military government.

Although one might have thought that peacetime conditions would have called for a new type of military governor, there was actually little difference between the political philosophies of Generals Brooke and Miles. Like Miles, Brooke also insisted on the primary supremacy of the occupying army. Indeed, in a gratuitous gesture of Americanization which must have offended every native Puerto Rican, he even ordered the spelling of the island's name to be changed to *Porto* Rico.

Despite what appears to have been an overbearing attitude, however, Brooke apparently did recognize at least some of the facts of Puerto Rican (or perhaps Porto Rican) life. He let it be known, for example, that he would not interfere with the normal working of the island's legal system—except when it was not compatible with American interests. He reopened the island's school system—although now ordering the study of English to be made a required subject. He kept the old Spanish tax setup basically intact—feeling that he would rather put up with the abuses that entailed than deal with a new and perhaps chaotic situation.

Brooke, in other words, seems to have been a mixed bag. There is little doubt that he was seriously trying to do his level best for the island. But there is also little doubt that he was sure he could judge what was "best" far more cogently than could the Puerto Ricans themselves.

He thought that the elected assembly—the *Diputación Provincial*—was both unnecessary and useless under the conditions of American occupation. On November 29, 1898, he did away with that legislative body which Puerto Rico had struggled so bitterly to gain from Spain. He did, on the other hand, permit the Council of Administration—with its Secretaries of Government, Justice, Finance, and Public Works—to continue. He transferred the responsibilities of the *Diputación* to the council.

With the direction that events were starting to take, however, there is little wonder that Luis Muñoz Rivera—who, as Secretary of Government, was a leading member of the Council—had one strongly specific suggestion about improving Puerto Rican-American relations. He thought that the occupation should be ended as quickly as possible.

General Brooke served as military governor for less than two months. But by the time he left for home, resentment against the United States was growing on all fronts.

This was certainly not all Brooke's fault. The brisk, self-confident Anglo-Saxons with their strange way of looking at things, their odd customs, and even (to the Spanish, at least) their half-pagan religion, were trying to force a whole new way of life on the islanders. The Puerto Ricans—being human—were not taking this well.

Still another nagging problem was the fast-maturing hostility between the ordinary U.S. soldier and the Puerto Rican man in the street. We have already noted that American men in uniform were emphatically not given a general license to have themselves a ball at Puerto Rican expense. But the very fact that they could not be hauled into island courts could not help encouraging them to commit the sort of excesses soldiers almost always tend to commit in an occupied country.

On December 6, 1898, General Brooke was replaced by Brigadier General Guy V. Henry, who turned out to be even more rigid and iron-handed than Brooke had been.

Henry started out well. One of his first actions was to introduce a new program for the island which included improvements in Puerto Rico's sanitation conditions, education, and police methods. But even then there were ominous signs. Henry was not going to stand for much native criticism and hinted broadly at new restrictions on press freedom.

These hints grew rapidly into out-and-out threats when the newspaper *La Democracia* dared to speculate editorially about an ultimate end to the military government. No newspaper was to be permitted to discuss the U.S. Army or the military government, General Henry responded angrily, unless reporting a proven news story.

La Democracia, it may be recalled, was the paper founded by Luis Muñoz Rivera as an organ of the Autonomist Party. With the 1897 agreement with Spain, that party split in two: A minority disapproved of the pact, which they believed would give Puerto Rico a government that would be autonomous in name only, while a large majority went along with the pact and Muñoz Rivera. At this time the minority group called itself the Pure and Orthodox Party and the majority—who were in favor of a tie-in with Spain's Liberal Party—took the name of the Liberal Fusionist Party.

After a temporary reconciliation, the two factions separated once more during the American occupation. The Liberal Fusionists became the Federal Party, which in turn became the Union Party in 1902. Former members of the Pure and Orthodox Party now called themselves the Republican Party.

With these and other changes of names, it is hard to keep the different political parties and what they stood for straight. For now, however, the important thing to remember is that—at the period under discussion—Luis Muñoz Rivera almost certainly represented the political thinking of the vast majority of aware Puerto Ricans. And where Muñoz Rivera stood, naturally, so stood his paper, *La Democracia.*

When General Henry threatened *La Democracia*, in other words, he was not merely threatening a newspaper. He was attacking the prevailing mood of the island.

The paper, under the direction of its editor, Mariano Abril, did not knuckle under to Henry's threats. For the next two months, Abril printed editorial after editorial which took issue both with Henry and with the entire United States occupation policy.

The United States, in the meantime, was tightening its grip on the island. New and stronger laws were passed on a variety of subjects. U.S. immigration regulations, for instance, were imposed on Puerto Rico. The island's police force was brought directly under the military governor. New tax measures were imposed.

Then, on February 6, 1899, a major blow came. General Henry dismissed the island's Council of Administration. It was not compatible, he claimed, with "American methods and progress."

The Council, which General Brooke had permitted to continue, was one of the few links left with representative government. Now this too was gone. Its different responsibilities were transferred to separate Departments of State, Justice, Finance, and Interior—all of which would be more directly under the general's control.

Muñoz Rivera saw this as a move to change the independent-minded Council into a U.S.-style cabinet, and resigned in protest. Other of the secretaries resigned also and demanded the return of a government which would more nearly represent the wishes of the Puerto Rican people.

Henry dismissed these protests as premature. They were a matter for the American Congress to take up, he said. He went on to form a new government along the lines he had favored.

While all this was going on, General Henry was also arranging to use the island's civil court system to suppress critical newspapers. *La Democracia* was censured by the courts and *La Metralla*, a paper published in Ponce, was suspended from further publication.

Perhaps seeing some handwriting on the wall, *La Democracia's* editor, Mariano Abril, found it expedient to leave Puerto Rico for Washington, where he continued to lobby for greater island independence. Shortly afterward, he was followed to the United States by his publisher, Muñoz Rivera.

In May of 1899, after putting into effect a whole spate of other new laws, General Henry left the island at his own request. He was replaced as governor-general by Brigadier General George W. Davis.

General Davis seems to have been a far more sympathetic man than his military predecessors. Indeed, despite the official line in Washington—which called for less Puerto Rican self-rule, rather than more—Davis believed that his basic task was to help prepare the island for eventual autonomy. In line with this overall viewpoint, he made a number of improvements in the island's political conditions—giving the courts more independence, for example, and gaining a much fairer deal for Spanish natives who had been unjustly discriminated against.

Well-intentioned as he might have been, however, Davis was still an American general carrying out the policies of his own government. In addition to this, he was as firmly convinced as the men who came before him that the Puerto Ricans were not *yet* equipped to govern themselves. Any experiment in real self-government, he believed, would have the bad results of exposing the islanders to the mercies of their own "unscrupulous" politicians.

If General Davis was benevolent, therefore, he was a benevolent despot. And as such, he naturally came into conflict with the native pride of the Puerto Ricans. It was probably, in part, as a consequence of this that Davis felt he could not afford to allow complete freedom of the press, but continued the past policies of military censorship.

The most positive aspects of General Davis's character came out after the great hurricane of August 8, 1899. This disastrous storm added to the normal poverty and horrible health conditions on the island by destroying most of Puerto Rico's food supply and wiping out some 80 per cent of that year's coffee crop.

At this point, actual starvation threatened a large proportion of Puerto Rico's population. Many of the rural workers fled to the cities with their families in search of help. But there was no help for them there. They squatted helplessly on the outskirts of the cities, giving birth to the squalid slums that were the shame of American Puerto Rico during the 1930's and 1940's, and which are still not entirely eliminated even today.

General Davis reacted promptly. He sent off immediate letters of sympathy to the various mayors throughout the island and, far more importantly, called on Washington for aid.

The War Department came through with more than $1 million in food, clothing, and medicine. But now the Army had to distribute all this in the face of washed-out roads and ruinous conditions. In order to facilitate the job of distribution, Davis divided the country into twelve military districts and made sure that the clothes and rations were given out even-handedly.

The damage in terms of human life and suffering was still severe. There is little doubt, however, that it would have been much worse were it not for Davis's combination of military efficiency and real humanity.

General Davis was the last U.S. military governor of Puerto Rico. By the time he had left office, in May of 1900, he had completely remodeled the island's government in the interest of more efficient management. He did away, for instance, with the Departments of State, Finance, and Interior, putting a number of bureaus in their place. Here again, we see American efficiency making enemies of the people it promised to help, instead of—as in the aftermath of the hurricane—making friends and creating goodwill.

General Davis, to sum up, appears to have been the highest caliber of military officer. But like the military governors in general, he was a mixed blessing.

Although certainly better equipped for his job than the generals who came before him, Davis seems to have suffered from many of their basic flaws. While wanting nothing but good for the Puerto Ricans, he too appears to have looked down on them and to have felt that they had to be brought up to the American "level" before they could be dealt with as equals.

It is a shame, considering his character—although, considering his paternalism, no surprise—that when General Davis did leave office, he left behind him still more hostility toward the United States. There were few flowers for the Americans, now, and no more hurrahs at all.

Now that the official military occupation was over, however, a new question remained for the island: Could a civilian governor do any better?

THIRTEEN

THE WASHINGTON ARENA

Although the rulings and actions of the different military governors were certainly of vital day-to-day importance to the Puerto Ricans, their future—and the future of their island—was really being determined more than fifteen hundred miles away in Washington, D.C.

It was in Washington, after all, that the War Department had its headquarters. It was there that the President and Congress made their decisions and held their deliberations. And it was to that city, therefore, that such prominent islanders as Luis Muñoz Rivera and Mariano Abril, on the one hand, and José J. Henna and Eugenio M. de Hostos, on the other, came to argue for their disparate viewpoints.

It was very difficult for the different factions of Puerto Rican patriots to get together. The former Autonomists were now split into Muñoz Rivera's Federal Party and the Republican Party (composed of former members of the Pure and Orthodox Party). The Federals were still hoping for some sort of limited autonomy which would include voting rights for Puerto Rican citizens, free trade with the United States, and a U.S.-style educational system. The island's Republicans wanted much the same thing. The fraternal bitterness between those two factions, however, having its roots back in the time of the deal with Spain, effectively prevented them from getting together.

The third side in the Puerto Rican political triangle was composed of former members of the Puerto Rican Section of the Cuban Revolutionary Party. As their United States representatives, such as De Hostos and Henna, made clear, they wanted nothing less than full self-determination. Puerto Rico, they insisted, was every bit as entitled to this as was Cuba. In an obvious reference to the American Declaration of Independence, they stated that the continuing military occupation of the island was depriving Puerto Ricans of their "natural" right to life, liberty, and the pursuit of happiness.

In the face of these conflicting demands from the island and conflicting advice at home, President McKinley appointed a commission to study the state of Puerto Rico— both currently and as it had been under the Spaniards.

The head of that commission was Dr. Henry K. Carroll, a highly respected Methodist minister. He and his fellow investigators were already at work when a second commission, to work independently of the first, was set up by the U.S. War Department. This was the so-called Insular Commission.

The fact that the military and civilian commissions reached two separate conclusions should come as no great shock. The Carroll Commission—to deliberately oversimplify—found that the island was capable of self-government. The Insular Commission found that it was not.

Although the members of Dr. Carroll's commission did feel that Puerto Rico should have some form of autonomy, however, they were not blind to the problems that this would probably entail. They were well aware, for example, that the political situation on the island was a volatile one, with the different political leaders highly mistrustful of each other.

But the commissioners also understood that, while the Puerto Ricans might have been dissatisfied with the treatment they had received from Spain, they were just as unhappy with the American military occupation. The basic feeling of the commission was that the only way to settle the situation on the island was to give the islanders the opportunity—at least in part—to work out their destiny for themselves.

The Insular Commission opposed the civilian one, not only in the conclusion it reached, but in almost every detail along the way. Instead of hostility toward the U.S.

occupation, the Insular Commission found the people "abundantly satisfied" with the Americans and even noted that the Puerto Ricans took every opportunity to express their loyalty to "the government which relieved them from Spain's oppression."

In addition, the Insular Commission found that social conditions on the island were—in the words of the old Viennese joke—serious, but not hopeless. Great poverty did exist, the Commission conceded, but there was no starvation. Even though the Commission report was written *before* the devastating hurricane of 1899, this assurance has a curious ring to it.

The Insular Commission did believe that certain improvements needed to be made in island conditions. But most of the proposals followed the general line of Americanization. The Commission found it far easier to recognize Spanish inequities, apparently, than the inequities involved with the United States military occupation.

For example, the Commission felt that Puerto Rico's criminal code—which was based on the European practice (derived, in turn, from old Roman law) of considering an accused man guilty until proven innocent—should be changed to one which made use of the traditional Anglo-American presumption of innocence. It also wished to change the Spanish-derived tax system.

One subject which both the Carroll Commission and the Insular Commission agreed on was the necessity for freer trade between Puerto Rico and the United States. And it was just this subject that was the cause of major debate on the floor of both houses of the United States Congress.

To a Puerto Rican, perhaps, the issue might have appeared to be a simple one: If the island now belonged to the United States, then it should have free access to American markets. What else could American hegemony mean?

But when it comes to politics, nothing is that simple. There were many voices raised both in Congress and throughout the land to make Puerto Rico a "nonincorporated" territory which would not be protected by the American Constitution and which would not be in a free trading area with the United States.

Of the voices in Congress, none was more forceful than that of an Ohio senator named Joseph Benson Foraker. Foraker was a strong fighter for the idea of Manifest

Destiny and American expansion. He had been one of the most vigorous supporters of the Spanish American War. Now that that war was won, he was the sponsor of a bill which would clamp down on Puerto Rican aspirations and which would permit the United States to rule the island with a strong hand.

But although Senator Foraker represented what was probably the point of view of most Americans, there was a body of Congressional opinion on the other side. The anti-Foraker viewpoint found its expression in a bill originating in the House of Representatives—one sponsored by Congressman Payne.

Payne's House committee was far more sensitive to Puerto Rican aspirations than was the Senate committee. It called many witnesses who were not only in favor of free trade between America and the island, but who were for Puerto Rican self-determination as well. One of these witnesses, the former separatist José J. Henna, complained that as things stood Puerto Ricans had neither civil rights nor political status. "We are Mr. Nobody from Nowhere," he said.

But the times were against political freedom for the island. Foraker had popular opinion on his side. He also had the powerful U.S. sugar, tobacco, and other agricultural interests who feared that they might be adversely affected if Puerto Rican products were permitted freely to invade the American market.

Furthermore, Foraker apparently truly believed what he said: that the Constitution had been drawn up to protect the people living within the continental boundaries of the United States, but not necessarily to protect residents of those territories newly annexed by the country. It was the duty of Congress alone to govern the new territories in any way it thought best, he claimed. The only restraint on Congress could come from its own sense of justice and from *specific* constitutional bans on its power.

"Is it possible," Foraker demanded rhetorically in the course of Senate debate, "that this great and powerful nation of ours, powerful in peace and powerful in war, and to be powerful, we trust, in the commercial world, has no power to subserve its own necessary and constitutional purposes except only by the consent of the people who may for the time being be affected? I utterly repudiate any such doctrine."

A great many Americans found themselves in strong

sympathy with the Senator's words. Who were the Puerto Ricans, anyway, to think that they could stand in the path of America's best interests? They were ignorant. Many of them were even illiterate. A few of their critics even suggested that they were "unmanly"—having let Spain oppress them for all those hundreds of years, they had no right now to demand self-government or even free trade with the United States.

The Foraker Act—officially called the Organic Act of 1900—passed.

One of the best things that can be said about the act, which was finally signed into law, is that it was not nearly as bad as it might have been. It did not justify the worst fears of the Puerto Ricans.

Although the act did constitute a step backward from the form of autonomy that Spain had given the island just before the United States take-over, it at least made a bow in the direction of self-government and future free trade. When the new civilian governor, Charles H. Allen, was inaugurated, George W. Davis, the outgoing military governor, was able to make a farewell speech in which he could assure the islanders that the Foraker Act promised them free trade with America just as soon as they were ready for it.

(There it was again, however. As soon as they were ready. A growing number of Puerto Ricans could not help feeling bitter whenever they heard that phrase. As far as they were concerned, they *were* ready—and had been ready for generations. It was first Spain and now the United States that was not ready.)

This time, though, the promise did have meaning. A tariff wall was put up between the United States and Puerto Rico. But the wall was to be removed either after the island's legislators had worked out a local tax system or by March 1, 1902—whichever came first. Actually, free trade with the United States was to come in another year, in 1901.

Politically, the act set up a two-chamber legislative body. The upper house had eleven members, five of whom were to be native Puerto Ricans. Six members of this body were to act as the island's cabinet. All the members of this house (called the Executive Council) were to be appointed by the U.S. President and consented to by the Senate in Washington.

The lower house was the thirty-five-man House of Delegates. The members were to be elected on the island by qualified voters.

The governor of the island—now a civilian—was to be a Presidential appointee. He was given the power to veto all legislation, although a two-thirds vote of *both* houses could override the veto.

Final and absolute power over the island, however, was still to be kept in Washington. Any and all laws passed in Puerto Rico were subject to nullification by the American Congress.

Although it might have been hard to believe at the time, one of the most ultimately beneficial sections of the act was that which provided for the island election of a resident commissioner who would be invited to go to Washington and sit in the U.S. Congress.

The commissioner was to be voteless, but not voiceless. Although he could not vote against legislation, he could protest against the bad and lobby for the good. He would be able to become, therefore, a constant gadfly— reminding Congress about the state of his island and refusing to permit Puerto Rico to become conveniently buried in a forest of generalities.

Most of the hostility against the Foraker Act arose from its underlying assumption that the U.S. Constitution did not protect the island or its people. The opposition to this came not only from Puerto Rico, but from many liberal elements in the United States itself. Some of the opponents, indeed, claimed that the Foraker Act was in itself unconstitutional.

The constitutional issue culminated in a celebrated court case, *Downs v. Bidwell*, which eventually wound up in the Supreme Court. In a five-to-four decision, the Court decided that Foraker had been right all along. The Constitution did not—at least in its entirety—automatically apply to newly acquired territories such as Puerto Rico.

In reaching this conclusion, the Justices explained that the Constitution had both fundamental guarantees—which did apply to all U.S. territories—and *non*fundamental guarantees. The nonfundamental guarantees (which surprisingly enough appeared to include the right to a trial by jury) would only apply to the new territories when Congress said they would. And in Puerto Rico's case, Congress had not yet said so.

Whether the Puerto Ricans liked it or not, therefore, the Foraker Act was the law of their island. It would remain the law for another seventeen years.

FOURTEEN

EARLY U. S. CIVILIAN RULE

The first American civilian governor, Charles H. Allen, was inaugurated on May 1, 1900, in San Juan. One of the earliest tasks on his agenda was to arrange for the elections called for under the Foraker Act.

This was to prove no easy task. The two major parties on the island—the Republican and the Federal—were not only in opposition, but bitterly jealous of any advantage that the other might have. And if, in the beginning at least, their mutual hatred was more personal than ideological, that did not make that hatred any less real.

The Executive Council—which had been chosen by the U.S. President under the law as stated by the Foraker Act—took on the job of dividing the island into different electoral districts and precincts. Even as this division was being made, however, the two major parties were feuding about it. And no sooner were the decisions announced than the Federal Party claimed—perhaps rightly—that it was being discriminated against.

Muñoz Rivera in particular believed that the Republicans had been favored as being more pro-United States than his own party. If the division had been done fairly, he said, the Federalists could have won a majority of districts without even having to campaign.

As for the Federal Party, it was accused of being a hotbed of anti-Americanism. The Republican leader, José Celso Barbosa, claimed also that Muñoz Rivera had dictatorial ambitions.

As the campaign atmosphere became hotter, both parties indeed began to solidify their separate positions. More and more, Muñoz Rivera and the other Federalists appealed to the people through their basic pride as Puerto Ricans, while Barbosa called for closer ties with the United States.

The longer the campaign dragged on, the more apparent it became that the Republicans—perhaps because of that disputed division of electoral districts—were going to win. Despite Muñoz Rivera's urgings to the contrary, the Federal Party pulled out of the elections while, at the same time, the two Federalist members of the cabinet resigned.

On September 14, 1900, the acrimony between the two parties exploded in dangerous riots. The Republicans claimed to be attacked by armed Federalists. The Federal story was that a Republican mob was out to get Luis Muñoz Rivera and the leader's friends had to form a bodyguard in order to protect him. Whatever the truth of the matter, the fracas ended with Muñoz Rivera and his friends being arrested for armed assault.

Although the judge who tried the case was a personal enemy of Muñoz Rivera, the Federal leader was acquitted. It has been claimed that if Muñoz Rivera had been found guilty, a general uprising by his followers would have taken place on the island.

Election day of November 6 came none too soon. With the Federal Party advising its supporters not to vote, the Republicans won in a walk. No matter who won the election, however, a good many islanders must have heaved a collective sigh of relief that the whole business was finally over.

But Puerto Rico's political problems were far from over. The old hatreds between the factions hung on. And the fires of those hatreds were further fanned by the fact that the island's economy was once more going steadily downhill.

American business, protected by the terms of the Foraker Act, was now starting to invest heavily in the island. Literally thousands of United States businessmen wished to take advantage of the island's surplus of manpower and lack of labor strife by putting their money into Puerto Rico. But the way these investments were being made hardly benefited the Puerto Ricans.

Even before the initial election under American rule

was completed, syndicates were formed to buy up the best land for growing sugar, coffee, and tobacco. Soon the very richest of Puerto Rico's farm land would be owned from afar and run, naturally enough, in a way most beneficial to the American owners.

Of all the island products that American industry was interested in, sugar was the most highly valued. The United States consumer was too accustomed to the coffee and tobacco grown on other soil to prefer the Puerto Rican product. But there was no way for him to tell the difference between Puerto Rican sugar and, say, sugar grown in Cuba.

The result of this economic fact of life was the gradual transfer of Puerto Rican lands into sugar plantations and the growing dependency of the island's economy on the sugar industry. What gold had once been, in other words, and what smuggling and privateering became, sugar was in the process of becoming.

This process did not take place overnight. But the handwriting was already on the wall. And by the year 1930, sugar exports were to make up about 65 per cent of all the goods exported from Puerto Rico, while the entire sugar industry was to compose some 78 per cent of the capital invested in island manufacturing.

This naturally meant that other industries were being squeezed out of existence. Most small farmers would not be able to earn a living. Nor would the coffee plantations, which—protected by the Spanish tariff—had done so well under Spain. The one-crop island would become even less self-sufficient than it had been in the past.

The new American tax setup was as protective of American-based businessmen as the old Spanish tax laws had been protective of merchants in Spain. This helped to increase the island's economic bind. Puerto Rico was forced to sell its sugar to American markets in order to buy what it needed at high U.S. prices. The average Puerto Rican, therefore, found himself paying more and more for less and less.

These economic factors hardly helped to improve the worsening feelings of Puerto Ricans toward the United States. As time went on, many islanders began to feel that they had merely exchanged one set of masters for another: Spanish autocrats for Yankee "carpetbaggers."

By the year 1901, conditions on the island were convincing a good number of Puerto Ricans to switch political sides. More and more of them were deserting the U.S.-oriented Republican Party, which they rightly or wrongly blamed for many of their troubles.

One newspaper to make this change was the *San Juan News*, an English-language paper which had been started in the early days of the U.S. occupation with the avowed purpose of representing the American viewpoint. The *News* had been in favor of the Republican Party, indeed, mainly because the paper felt that it was more pro-American than the Federal. Now, however, it was chiding the U.S.-appointed governor for not cooperating closely enough with the Federal Party, which the paper claimed represented a majority on the island.

The *News* editorial writers were among those upset by what they foresaw of coming economic events. Realizing that, under the new tax laws, the balance of trade would necessarily favor the United States, the *News* claimed that sugar and coffee would monopolize most of the island's trade. (The paper was right about sugar, as we have seen, although wrong about coffee.) Furthermore, the paper's editorial writer understood, most of the profits from these industries would probably be withdrawn from Puerto Rico.

Another problem which was adding to Puerto Rico's social woes was what the *News* termed "landlordism." Enormous rents were making a few people extremely wealthy, while most of the islanders lived in abject poverty. An apartment in San Juan, the paper charged, could cost up to five times as much as the same apartment in New York City.

In the face of all this, it would have been a miracle if anger and bitterness did not continue to rise. No such miracle happened. When Governor Charles H. Allen told a Boston newspaper reporter that Puerto Rico was a lucky island because it had no public debts and its taxes were large enough to cover its budget, the statement might well have reassured Bostonians. Puerto Ricans who read about it, however, could be expected to feel enraged.

One of those who was angered by that statement was Luis Muñoz Rivera, who answered it in his new weekly newspaper, *Puerto Rico Herald*. On this "lucky island," Muñoz Rivera retorted savagely, many people were faced with the choice of starvation or emigration to Cuba, Ecuador, or Hawaii. Puerto Rico *should* have a public debt, Muñoz Rivera maintained. The island's "good credit standing should be used to put money into circulation and to rebuild its agriculture. As for the taxes with which we balance our budget, Governor Allen does not seem to care how he mows wheat in the field of a stranger, whose ruin is not important."

These are strong and—even over a bridge of years—poignant words. They could not have been used only a few years before. But in 1904 Muñoz Rivera would use language that was even stronger: "In 1901, only a few of us distrusted the United States," he wrote in the *Herald*. "Today all are beginning to realize that we have been deceived. We no longer worship everything that comes from the North."

Muñoz Rivera and his fellow Federalists were not the only islanders to feel anger and bitterness. A good many Republicans were starting to move to the left in a revolt against their own leadership. One of these was Santiago Iglesias Pantín, a young and fiery Spaniard with socialist leanings. Iglesias was helping to organize Puerto Rican labor into a strong and militant force for the first time.

In his later career, Iglesias would work to form a Socialist Party on the island—one that was unaffiliated, however, with the international Socialist movement. Still later, he would become a "respectable" labor diplomat and would even be elected to the Washington-based job of Puerto Rican resident commissioner in 1932. But in the early days of American control, Iglesias' name was anathema—both to the U.S. authorities and to many of his then fellow Republicans on the island.

When Iglesias was thrown into jail following his participation in labor conflicts, some Puerto Ricans suspected that this was done to remove his influence on the Republican Party. Whether or not this was the case, support for Iglesias grew all over the island. His imprisonment became symbolic of what was least liked about the American occupation.

FIFTEEN

INCHING TOWARD DEMOCRACY

In the year 1904 the political party of Luis Muñoz Rivera opened its ranks to a large number of dissident Republicans and, at the same time, changed its name from the Federal Party to the Unionist Party—*Unión de Puerto Rico*.

The platform of this well-established although newly reconstituted party discussed several alternative solutions to the island's problems. One alternative which the Unionists found acceptable was that of island independence. This was an enormous change for a party founded by former Autonomists. It meant that political leaders who had always tried their best to avoid a separate path for the island would now prefer that to the way things were going. More self-government was what the Unionists wanted—and whether they gained it through statehood, by means of autonomy, or through independence did not seem to matter much anymore.

The Republican Party wanted more self-rule also. They traced their seven-year history, after all, back to the same Autonomist movement that the Unionists did. The Republicans, however, did not believe it desirable to change their basically pro-American position.

Most Republican Party members believed that much more could be done for the island by working within the system. Rather than oppose the United States and hold out for what they felt they couldn't get, they thought it would be wiser to proclaim their loyalty and work for slow change.

But while the Republican position had won support in the recent past, it did not have a chance in 1904. This year, the electorate was expanded in order to bring voting regulations more in line with those in the United States. Every male over the age of twenty-one, whether or not he could read and write, was now permitted to vote in the elections. The poverty-stricken residents of the cities could vote. The *jíbaros*—the mountain-bred, who were possibly even worse off than the city dwellers—could vote. And all of them—all those who felt themselves abused by the United States—voted to express their anger in the only way they were permitted to: for the Unionist Party.

It was a landslide. The Unionists picked up almost 90,000 votes, while the Republicans could only gather about 54,000.

And this was to continue. In 1906 and 1908 the Unionists won again, with even greater majorities. In the year 1910 approximately 100,000 people voted for Unionist candidates, while a mere 59,000 voted for the still pro-American Republicans.

There could be little question now about where the sympathies of the average Puerto Rican lay. Anti-Americanism was not a mere political fad, it was a basic fact of island life. When a Puerto Rican intellectual stated, in 1910, that the island "has no motive . . . to be thankful to or to care for the American people, who have done everything possible to keep us from caring for them," he was expressing the viewpoint shared by a large percentage of his fellow countrymen.

And yet, no matter how unwelcome, the facts were still the facts. The Republicans did have a point. The United States certainly appeared to be on the island to stay. Puerto Rico was apparently going to have to find some way of gaining more self-determination while still getting along with the new mother country.

In the meantime, it should also not be thought that no Americans made any attempt to improve conditions on the island. Both the government in Washington and private U.S. charities had been making and would continue to make strong attempts to solve specific problems. While some of these efforts came to nothing, others were of real value.

One of the earliest attempts to control the land-grabbing activities of the American syndicates, for example, came on May 1, 1900, when the United States Congress enacted a supplement to the Foraker Act, which had passed into law less than a month before. The supplement took the form of a joint resolution prohibiting any corporation from owning more than five hundred acres of Puerto Rican land. It was specifically designed to prevent a small number of corporate landlords from controlling all or most of the island's best agricultural land.

Unfortunately, this was one of the attempts to help the island that came to nothing. No law, whether it be bad or good, can do anything unless it is capable of being enforced. And it was held that Puerto Rico had no legal or constitutional right to enforce the resolution on land limitation. So the unenforceable law stayed on the books until 1940, when the U.S. Supreme Court handed down a decision which held that the island's legislature did indeed have the power to enforce it.

America did far better in the fields of public works and island health.

A network of new roads was built on the island in order to improve transportation and communications. Public utilities, power plants, and other municipal works were also constructed.

Sanitation conditions were upgraded, especially in San Juan. By the year 1914, in fact, that city had earned the reputation of being one of the cleanest metropolises in the world. The island's educational system was vastly improved after the American occupation, and illiteracy was sliced in half within a single generation.

Private charities, foundations, and church organizations did their best to help out also. Protestant church groups supported hospitals, the most noteworthy of which was probably the San Juan Presbyterian. The Rockefeller Foundation sent teams of scientists to combat malaria and hookworm. The American Red Cross founded a program to provide public nursing care for the rural interior.

But all these efforts, plus many others which came both early and late, were hardly solving the island's major problems.

By 1909 the political situation on the island was such that both political parties agreed that one of the largest stumbling blocks in the path of Puerto Rican development was the Foraker Act. Both Muñoz Rivera and the Republican Party leader, José C. Barbosa, appeared together in public and pledged to work toward its repeal.

In the Unionist landslide of 1910, Muñoz Rivera won the position of resident commissioner. This presented him with the opportunity, in effect, of putting the opposition party's theories into practice. He would now have a chance to work within the system. Once stationed in Washington, he might be able to make a dent in the Foraker Act.

But how? Muñoz Rivera was faced with a dilemma. Not only understanding the growing impatience of his fellow islanders, but sharing it as well, he still had to get what he could. No matter what he wanted for Puerto Rico in the long run—probably independence—the best he could hope for at present was some kind of internal autonomy. His strategy would be to use Puerto Rican impatience as a political lever. If you refuse us autonomy now, he would imply to government officials, we may soon demand independence.

In his attempts to work with the Washington lawmakers, Muñoz Rivera had two fundamental problems. The first was that his command of the English language was poor. In writing the English articles for his *Puerto Rican Herald*, he had been forced to use translators. But in the give and take of political discussion, a translator would be a real handicap. So, at the age of fifty-one, he bent his efforts to the study of English.

This first problem was at least a fairly straightforward one. Annoying as it was, it could still be solved by sheer hard work. His second problem was political—and therefore much more difficult.

Muñoz Rivera's Unionist Party of Puerto Rico was affiliated with the Democratic Party in the United States. But when Muñoz Rivera came to Washington as resident commissioner, he found a Republican administration in which William Howard Taft was President. How was the leader of a Democratic Party affiliate going to convince a Republican administration to give him what he wanted?

The answer is the obvious one. He didn't. Even though the (U.S.) Republican Party had been defeated in the Congressional elections of 1910.

In 1912, however, the former Republican President, Theodore Roosevelt, ran for the presidency as the candidate of the newly formed splinter group, the Progressive or "Bull Moose" Party. Although losing, he came in ahead

of Taft and made such a split in the Republican vote that
the Democrat, Woodrow Wilson, was elected. At the same
time, a number of Progressive Party candidates were
placed in Congress.

With the Progressive reform movement at a high tide in
the United States, and with a Democrat in the White
House, Muñoz Rivera found himself in a much better
position to do something for Puerto Rico.

All of this, however, might still not have done the trick
were it not for the onset of World War I. But with
German diplomats making strong efforts to woo Latin
America away from the United States sphere of influence, a good many Washington officials thought it woul.
make sense to improve the American "image" by granting
more self-determination to the country's major Latin pos
session.

In 1916, therefore, a Democratic Congressman from
Virginia, William A. Jones, sponsored a bill to replace the
Foraker Act. It would give Puerto Rico far more control
over its own internal affairs than before, and would at last
make the islanders citizens of the United States.

The new bill came almost too late to have a real effect
on Puerto Rican attitudes. A left-wing faction of the
Unionist Party promptly condemned it as being an instru-
ment of colonialism. Under the leadership of José de
Diego, a poet-intellectual, this faction was demanding
nothing less than immediate independence.

The "independence now" faction was especially
incensed by the clause in the Jones Act which stated that
American citizenship would be "imposed" on the island.
Accepting this, it felt, would mean that Puerto Rico would
never gain its independence.

Whether a majority of Puerto Ricans of the time did or
did not want total independence is open to question. But
even if they did, the United States was not about to grant
it. As Muñoz Rivera and his associates realized, it would
be the Jones Act or nothing.

Therefore, although he apparently had his own doubts
about the advantages of citizenship, Muñoz Rivera disregarded the outraged left wing of his own party and flung
himself wholeheartedly into the effort to convince Congress to pass the new bill. Using his recently gained
knowledge of English to amazingly good effect, he met
privately with Congressmen, attended committee meet-

ings, and spoke on the floor of the House of Representatives.

There can be no doubt that Muñoz Rivera's tremendous effort was one of the deciding factors in the passage of the Jones Act through the House of Representatives in 1916. But there can be no doubt, either, that this expenditure of energy helped to ruin his health. In September of 1916, with the Jones Bill still not voted on by the Senate, he decided to leave Washington for a while in order to take a much needed rest in Puerto Rico.

Once back on the island, Muñoz Rivera headed for his home in Barranquitas, the lovely mountain town where he was born. There he hoped to relax and regain the strength to fight the battles that were still ahead. He was never to leave Barranquitas again, for he died there on November 16, 1916.

Muñoz Rivera's former home in that town, which is now about an hour and a half drive from the city of San Juan, has been turned into a library and museum. It is open to the public.

On March 2, 1917, the Jones Act was signed into law.

The new bill had many positive aspects. It gave Puerto Rico a bill of rights in line with those enjoyed in the continental United States. Like the Foraker Act, it provided for a legislature with two chambers. But now *both* houses would be chosen through universal suffrage of all males over the age of twenty-one.

The citizenship question also appeared to be resolved. The completed law gave the Puerto Ricans the choice of rejecting American citizenship. When it came to the test, incidentally, only 288 out of the total population voted to turn citizenship down.

But still, there were plenty of objections—plenty of people who felt that the Jones Act made only a minimum gesture in the direction of self-rule.

Representative Jones himself has been reported as admitting that the island's new constitution had been deliberately designed to hold down the power of the popularly elected legislature. And if that weren't enough, a veto power over new laws was still retained by both the island's Washington-appointed governor and the President of the United States.

The Supreme Court Justices, furthermore, as well as three of the most important cabinet members—the attorney general, the auditor, and the commissioner of education—would continue to be appointed from Washington.

Was the Jones Act a phony, then? Did it merely pretend to do something in order to make good propaganda for the United States and keep the Puerto Ricans quiet?

The answer to a question like that naturally has to depend on one's point of view. But practically speaking, Muñoz Rivera was probably right. It was just about the very best that could have been gotten at the time. And—although not as large a move toward island democracy as many Puerto Ricans would have wanted—it *was* a move.

No one can deny, on the other hand, that with just a little more goodwill, the Jones Act could have been much, much better than it was.

SIXTEEN

INTO THE TWENTIES

There was not a great deal of real difference in the life of the island as it was lived under the new Jones Act and the way it had been lived under the Foraker Act. Puerto Rico was still poverty-stricken. Its inhabitants were still in deep trouble.

It also continued to be an unincorporated territory—"at the mercy of the American Congress," as the writer Cayetano Coll y Toste had put it back in 1908.

This question of incorporation was finally settled in 1922. Before then, some Puerto Ricans continued to hope that passage of the Jones Act was an indication that the island was not to be treated on an equal basis with the incorporated territories of Alaska and Hawaii, for example—both of which were confidently expected to reach statehood sooner or later. But in 1922 a U.S. Supreme Court decision ruled that nothing had changed in the basic relationship between Puerto Rico and the United States.

The Puerto Rican people, the Court pointed out in the case of *Balzac v. Porto Rico,* continued to live in their own ancient communities according to their long-established customs. Even though the island might belong to the United States, therefore, it could not be considered as incorporated into it. That this same argument could well be used in favor of the island's independence, incidentally, was not mentioned in the Court's opinion.

Some more cynical Americans felt—as they still do feel—that this decision actually did the Puerto Ricans a favor since residents of unincorporated territories do not have to pay federal taxes. But it was a tremendous blow to the island's pride. It should also be mentioned that the tax-haven aspects could only be taken advantage of by the comparatively few islanders who were members of the middle and upper classes—plus, of course, any mainlanders who came there for that purpose. The average Puerto Rican was far too poor to have to worry about taxes.

As an American possession, whether incorporated or unincorporated, Puerto Rico was naturally expected to do its part in the war against Germany, which the United States officially entered in April of 1917. The island did. It registered more than 100,000 males and called up nearly 13,000 of them by the following November.

The war was forcefully brought home to the island long before November, however. On June 2, 1917, the passenger ship *Carolina* of the Porto Rico Line was torpedoed on the run between San Juan and New York. Though only sixteen lives were lost when the ship went down, the island was terrified about what this might bode for the future. If the sea link between Puerto Rico and the United States could be cut, the island's food supply—a large part of which came from America—would be drastically curtailed.

New island laws were passed, however, promoting the production of local food crops. With land being placed under cultivation for food production, Puerto Rico gained a small measure of self-sufficiency. What was apparently impossible in peacetime could be done in time of war.

Temporarily, at least, World War I helped the island's economy. But at war's end Puerto Rico found itself in worse shape than it had been before.

The sugar industry in particular was in a state of complete collapse, with prices for that product dropping abruptly from twenty-three cents a pound to four cents. As Puerto Rico was practically a "sugar island" by now, this meant severe dislocation and unemployment for the great mass of the population.

The island government did what it could. It poured literally millions of dollars into such projects as hospitals, schools, hydroelectric plants, and bridge building in order to partially take up the slack. New industries were also started at this time. The needlework industry, which was used to give work to women, is an example of this.

But none of these efforts was enough to halt the growing discontent of the people—especially the people of the interior, who were hurt most by the collapse of sugar and helped least by the government's efforts to combat its effects.

The *jíbaro*—the man born and bred in the island's mountain country—has always liked to consider himself as the "real" Puerto Rican. He was and still is more self-supporting than his city-dwelling cousin, and even grows a few food crops on his tiny plot of land. The *jíbaro's* main income, however, must always come from the coffee or tobacco or sugar plantation where he is employed.

According to those who have known him, the true *jíbaro* is a decent and patient man whose warmth and hospitality are practically legendary. Throughout the years, he has suffered even more than most Puerto Ricans from overwork, malnutrition, ill-health, and the often violent forces of nature.

Most experts on the island agree that the *jíbaro* is fast disappearing from the Puerto Rican scene. He will not be found at all, they say, within another generation or two, but will be amalgamated into the general mix of the lower middle class. At the time which we are now considering, though, he was an important political force on the island.

In the late teens and the early twenties, the *jíbaro* found himself disillusioned with both the Republican and the Unionist Parties. Neither one was doing anything for him. That being the case, he was drawn to a political group founded in 1908 as the Workers Party and which, in 1910, became the Socialist Party.

The leader of the Socialists was the former left-wing Republican Santiago Iglesias Pantín. With the help of the *jíbaros,* Iglesias was elected in 1920 as the first Socialist senator. The Socialist Party as a whole received one fourth of the total vote cast in that election.

During this period, the son of Luis Muñoz Rivera was living in New York City, where he was writing a series of articles about Puerto Rico for such United States publications as H. L. Mencken's *Smart Set*, the *New Republic*, and *The Nation*.

Luis Muñoz Marín had been born in San Juan, but

came to America with his father in 1919, when he was twelve years old. Muñoz Marín was educated in the public school systems of New York and Washington, D.C. After attending Georgetown University, he became a poet and journalist and—while still making his home in the United States—was increasingly concerned with island problems.

Considering his family name, it is not surprising that Puerto Rican political leaders were concerned with him. And when, on a trip to the island, he met Santiago Iglesias, the Socialist leader took pains to convert Muñoz Marín to his own way of thinking.

He did not stay converted long, however. In 1924 a coalition between the Socialists and certain of the Republicans—that faction known as the Constitutional Historical Party—made the young Muñoz wonder if there were any real differences between the parties, or if they weren't all just out for political gain. He withdrew his Socialist affiliation.

Muñoz Marín returned to the island in 1926. He took over the editorship of his father's old paper, *La Democracia*. In that position he could write editorials which attacked Puerto Rican conditions in general and the political power structure in particular. Perhaps, also, he was brooding about a future in which he might start a new political party of his own.

The Puerto Rican economy, in the meanwhile, had still not recovered from the collapse of the sugar industry. Wages were down all over the island. Employment was off. Profits were practically nonexistent.

What was to be done? Missions were sent to the United States in order to try to obtain new and more diversified private investments in the island. But the missions— including the one that Muñoz Marín was sent on in 1927—were failures.

In America this was the era of the "Roaring Twenties." Why should any businessman wish to take the risk of building new industries in nonindustrialized Puerto Rico when investments made in the United States proper were sure to bring such high rewards?

During 1926 and 1927 there were only a couple of island events worth getting excited about. The first of these, in 1926, was the opening of a School of Tropical Medicine. The project, jointly sponsored by Columbia

University in New York and the University of Puerto Rico in San Juan, was the first school of tropical medicine to be founded anywhere in the Americas.

The event of 1927 was more festive—though not nearly as important. This was the visit of Charles Lindbergh, who flew to the island from St. Croix on February 2.

Lindbergh was on a triumphant flying tour with his *Spirit of St. Louis,* the single-engine airplane in which he had flown the Atlantic Ocean from New York to Paris alone. The Puerto Rican people gave him a hero's welcome. But the president of the Senate and the speaker of the House wanted to use this visit to help the island. Perhaps Colonel Lindbergh would intercede for them with the U.S. President, Calvin Coolidge, and deliver a message asking for more self-rule. Puerto Rico still wanted an elective governor.

Coolidge's answer was to the point. It can also serve as a good example of typical American opinion of that day: "The United States," the President replied, "has made no promise to the people of Puerto Rico that has not been more than fulfilled."

In September of 1928, a new hurricane caused further havoc with the island's agricultural situation. This time, the fruit and coffee industries were completely ruined. A few weeks after this storm, the losses from it were estimated to be approximately $85 million—which made it the greatest loss in Puerto Rico's history. Congress later gave $6 million to the island in order to help repair some of the damage.

In March of 1929, about six months after the hurricane, the leaders of the Republican and Socialist Parties of Puerto Rico joined ranks to ask Herbert Hoover, the newly inaugurated American President, to authorize a loan of $100 million in order to provide a program of health, education, and industrialization, and also to repay public indebtedness.

One cannot know what went through President Hoover's mind when he received this plea. But in just a few more months, he would be weighted down by many more problems than Puerto Rico's.

October 29, 1929, marked the beginning of the stock market crash. The era of United States prosperity had come to a sickening halt, and the Great Depression was at hand.

SEVENTEEN

DEPRESSION YEARS

"When the United States catches cold," a friend on the island once told me, "Puerto Rico sneezes."

And during the Great Depression of the 1930's, the United States caught far worse than a simple cold. It suffered a grave disorder that many at the time feared it might never recover from. Poverty was rampant from one coast to the other. Family homes, farms, and businesses were placed on the block at sheriff's sales. Formerly prosperous men and women counted themselves lucky to find a street corner where they could sell apples or pencils. President Franklin Delano Roosevelt's well-known description of one third of the nation being ill-clothed, ill-housed, and ill-fed was not mere rhetoric but a statement of fact.

And in Puerto Rico? In Puerto Rico conditions were even worse than they were on the continent. If the island continued to suffer during America's healthy years, the illness of America produced greater suffering still.

One Depression visitor to Puerto Rico was Harold L. Ickes, the controversial American Secretary of the Interior during the Roosevelt administration. On a 1936 inspection tour of the island, Ickes was taken to two or three of San Juan's slum areas, which he described as the very worst he had ever seen. He confided his shock and outrage to his private diary (published in Volume I of *The Secret Diary of Harold L. Ickes,* New York, 1953).

"The dwellings," he wrote, "looked as if a breath would

129

blow them over. They are thoroughly disreputable and disagreeable. Open sewage runs through the streets and around the buildings and there are no sanitary facilities at all. The children play in this sewage, which in many cases is covered with a thick, green scum. The houses appear to be dirty and unkempt. The cooking is done on little charcoal stoves, and the furniture is of the simplest and scantiest. Notwithstanding these terrible conditions, generally speaking, the people in the slums, and especially the younger women, had the appearance of being neat and clean, although I cannot see how they can possibly be clean, considering the surroundings in which they live. Such slums are a reflection not only upon the Puerto Rican Government but upon that of the United States. It is unbelievable that human beings can be permitted to live in such noisome cesspools."

Unbelievable or not, there the slum dwellers stayed. And the improvements made in those conditions during the period of the thirties came with agonizing slowness.

Not that nobody attempted to help. Sincere efforts were made from the very start of the epoch. But for one reason or another—because the trouble was deeply rooted, because of the political situation on the island and on the mainland, because the United States had too many of its own problems to concentrate properly on those of Puerto Rico—they mostly went awry.

In the year 1930 the Brookings Institution of Washington published an extensive socio-economic study of Puerto Rico's past and current situation which also made recommendations concerning the island's future. The Brookings report, entitled *Porto Rico and Its Problems,* was studied carefully by later agencies trying to attack the island's troubles.

Generally speaking, the Brookings Institution recommended administrative changes which would be designed to run the island more efficiently, plus an extension of stateside federal aid to Puerto Rico.

The report, incidentally, recalled the days of World War I, when the island had temporarily become far more self-sufficient in terms of growing its own food. Although that state of affairs might be socially desirable, the report concluded, it appeared to be economically unworkable. Puerto Rico's land could produce more income for its owners when used to grow the three major export crops of sugar, tobacco, and coffee.

In 1932 a couple of political events took place that were going to affect Puerto Rico during the coming years. In America Franklin D. Roosevelt was elected President and began planning his "New Deal" program. On the island itself Luis Muñoz Marín made a triumphant reentry into local politics.

At the conclusion of his unsuccessful mission to the United States in 1927. Muñoz decided to stay on for a while with his wife and family. He remained in America through the stock market crash and the beginning of the Depression, and did not return to Puerto Rico until August of 1931.

Once back on the island he became interested in a new political party that was preaching the doctrine of independence. This was the Liberal Party, which was currently in the process of being organized by the former head of the Unionists, Antonio R. Barceló.

Getting in on the ground floor, as it were, Muñoz became a candidate for the Puerto Rican Senate and won in the 1932 elections.

Roosevelt's New Deal, in the meantime, was casting about for the best means to fulfill its responsibilities to the island which America had taken over in 1898.

In 1933 Roosevelt established the Puerto Rican Emergency Relief Administration—thus taking a step in line with the Brookings report's recommendation of extending federal aid to the island. The PRERA was initially funded with a credit of $900,000.

Even in those days, however, this sum was a drop in the bucket. And furthermore, pure relief would not begin to solve the long-encrusted problems of the island. In 1934, therefore, the Puerto Rico Policy Commission, composed of island intellectual leaders under the chairmanship of Dr. Carlos Chardón, was called to Washington and asked to present a program to change the basic social and economic structure of the island.

According to the Commission's report, the basic problem in Puerto Rico—as far as the majority of its people were concerned, at least—could be reduced "to the simple terms of progressive landlessness, chronic unemployment, and implacable growth of the population. A policy of fundamental reconstruction should, therefore, contemplate the definite reduction of unemployment to a point, at least, where it may be adequately dealt with by normal relief agencies; and the achievement of this, largely by restoration of the land to the people that cultivate it, and by the fullest development of the industrial possibilities of the island."

This was political dynamite—especially the part which urged "restoration of the land to the people who cultivate it." More specifically, the Chardón Plan, as it became known, called for a segment of the powerful sugar industry to be publicly operated in a manner which would allow it to share profits with workers and farmers.

In suggesting this, the Chardón Plan followed an early proposal by Rexford G. Tugwell, a former professor of economics and one of the original "Brain Trusters," who became an undersecretary of agriculture in 1934. Chardón and his commission, indeed, did not go as far as Tugwell—who wished to socialize the entire industry and run it as a collective. As far as the plantation owners were concerned, though, Chardón went much too far.

But President Roosevelt looked upon the Chardón Plan with a good deal of sympathy. His own sympathetic feelings toward the island had been partly shaped by his wife's visits there and her personal reports to him. Now, in 1934, he visited Puerto Rico to examine conditions there for himself.

In the same month that the Puerto Rico Policy Commission was presenting its report, Roosevelt created a new division in the Department of the Interior—the Division of Territories and Island Possessions—and transferred responsibility for Puerto Rican affairs to it. This was the first time since the U.S. Army had landed on the island that the responsibility was not in the hands of the War Department.

Ernest Gruening, a former editor who had turned to government work, was given the position of director of the Division of Territories. In May of 1935 he was also appointed as the director of the Puerto Rico Reconstruction Administration. Part of this latter job consisted of administering the Chardón Plan.

Gruening's program included a breaking up of the vast sugar estates in accord with the law which had been enacted back in 1900 as a supplement to the Foraker Act—and had been ignored ever since. The first court case challenging the new enforcement policy dragged through Puerto Rican courts until 1938. It was finally settled in favor of the law by the U.S. Supreme Court decision of 1940.

Despite his strong sympathies for the island, Gruening had his work cut out for him. For one thing, every state on the mainland was competing for federal relief dollars. And as Puerto Rico would have no voice in United States elections, the mainland continued to have first call on money.

Under these circumstances, it is perhaps surprising that the Puerto Rico Reconstruction Administration accomplished as much as it did. More—and less expensive— electrical power was made available to the islanders at this time, much rural reconstruction and reforestation was accomplished, and new and better roads were built. New housing was put up during this period also. In San Juan today, in fact, an American visitor will be shown housing projects and proudly informed that they were "built by" Mrs. Roosevelt.

The problem—and so far in the story, at least, it has always seemed to be the problem with aid to Puerto Rico—was that not enough was done. What had started out as a major attack on underlying causes gradually became a treatment of symptoms.

It was a sincere treatment, given by men of goodwill. At times it was even an effective treatment. But those underlying causes remained.

A good part of the trouble lay in the fact that the administrators of the Chardón Plan faced the active hostility of Puerto Rico's major moneyed interests, which were the prime support of the established political parties. It might be too much to state that the parties of that era were actually on the payroll of the sugar growers, for example—but it would not be so terribly wide of the mark, at that.

This helps explain the fact that, while most of the political leaders cheered the inauguration of the Puerto Rico Reconstruction Administration, they soon stopped cooperating with it.

The political situation naturally disgusted a great percentage of the Puerto Rican people, who reacted in different ways to it. A small but increasingly noisy minority rallied around the new pro-Fascist and anti-American Nationalist Party, which demanded immediate independence in the most violent of terms.

The Nationalists were headed by Pedro Albizu Campos, a black man who has been termed both a fanatic and a political genius. Albizu had attended Harvard University in the United States. While there, he had suffered racial slurs and indignities that had turned him completely against America. Now he was preaching violence and telling his followers to arm themselves. Although his party could only garner some five thousand votes in the election of 1932, it managed to become a symbol of all the frustration and helpless anger on the island.

Still and all, the Nationalist episode might have remained hardly worth mentioning were it not for a tragedy which took place in February of 1936. But when a group of party members murdered the island's young police chief, Colonel E. Francis Riggs, they set in motion a train of other destructive events.

The police themselves shot down Riggs's killers. But island authorities also decided to crack down on the party and threw several of its leaders into jail.

The rank-and-file Nationalists protested their leaders' jailings all over the island. One protest parade was held in the city of Ponce, on Palm Sunday of 1937. Even though permission was granted by the mayor, the police were ready and waiting for the demonstrators—who included among their ranks young men from some of the most prominent families of the area. In apparent revenge for the murder of their popular chief, they opened fire on what has been reported to be an unarmed crowd. When the "Ponce Massacre"—as it has become known—was over, nineteen people were killed and many more wounded.

Taken together, the Riggs murder and the Ponce Massacre had a sobering effect on U.S.-Puerto Rican relations. They aroused ugly suspicions in both places and made the two parties even more suspicious of each other than they had ever been before.

What the Nationalist movement did accomplish, ironically, was the very opposite of what it had in mind. The murder of Colonel Riggs helped persuade Washington to perpetrate a political trick which killed the idea of island independence for many years to come.

After the killing of the police chief, President Roosevelt

wondered if it might not be a clever idea to permit Puerto Rico to have a plebiscite on the independence question. He brought up the question of introducing a bill in Congress to this effect in a meeting of his Cabinet.

"I expressed myself as being strongly in favor of such a bill," Secretary of the Interior Ickes wrote in his diary. "I pointed out that if Puerto Rico wanted its independence, it ought to be granted it, but if it should vote against independence, then such agitation as has been going on in Puerto Rico recently would be put an end to for probably twenty years."

Ickes explained his reasoning this way: "There is a bad situation in Puerto Rico. The chief of police was assassinated recently and two or three local officials were killed. There is reason to believe that there is a general plot to assassinate other island officials, including the governor. . . . I strongly urged [the proposed bill's] immediate introduction, although it might not pass at this session of the Congress because of the quieting effect that I anticipated it might have on Puerto Rican public opinion. I told the President that we had drafted such a bill in my Department and he authorized me to send it to Senator Tydings, with the suggestion that he introduce it, although not as an Administration bill."

Most of the other cabinet members concurred in this advice. And more importantly, so did the President. Tydings himself proved very willing to cooperate, especially as the murdered Colonel Riggs happened to be an old friend of his.

The result of these machinations was the Tydings Bill of 1936. It called for an island plebiscite of independence—but added several stipulations: If independence were to be chosen, it would have to come immediately. All United States aid to the island would then come to a halt. Furthermore, a 25 per cent tax would be promptly applied to all Puerto Rican sugar coming into the United States.

On the island, the Nationalists and Liberals predictably announced themselves in favor of the bill. The Nationalists wanted independence at any cost, while the Liberals believed that this kind of offer was all that Puerto Rico could ever expect to get from the United States.

But although no one on the island realized that the "Tydings" Bill actually originated with Roosevelt and his Cabinet, there were those who understood that the particular independence package they were offered was deliberately sabotaged. The United States had helped place Puerto Rico in the economic bind it was presently in, they believed. It should not be allowed to evade its responsibilities to the island by setting it adrift.

One leader who felt strongly about this was Luis Muñoz Marín, who parted company with his fellow liberal Antonio R. Barceló over this issue. While still insisting that he wanted independence, Muñoz did not want it under the threat of starvation. Independence had to be coupled with the kind of economic guarantees that would permit the island to live with dignity.

In the end, the Tydings Bill was turned down by the U.S. Senate, and the arguments in Puerto Rico were thus made academic. There was to be no plebiscite over independence.

By this time, however, the break between Muñoz and the majority of the Liberals was irreparable. Muñoz was on the way to organizing a new party of his own. Under his leadership, the Popular Democratic Party—*El Partido Popular Democrático*—was to achieve goals which would have been considered fantastic during the time of the great plebiscite debate.

EIGHTEEN

THE POPULAR MOVEMENT

In the meantime, however, the Great Depression dragged on. Year followed dreary year in a seemingly unending procession of darkness and misery, and the best efforts of sympathetic administrators working with New Deal aid could not hold back the waves of hopelessness which washed over the island. With a few exceptions, living conditions were still unbearable. Hunger was commonplace and poverty had become a way of life.

In 1938, therefore, when Luis Muñoz Marín decided to form his new political party, he knew that he would have to rethink his basic positions in order to come up with a new and distinct program.

Until this time, Muñoz Marín's political thinking had followed that of his father. He had made eventual independence his basic goal and measured all intermediate steps by whether or not they tended to further that aim. Events could force him to take a circuitous route—or even to take a seeming step backward, as his father had done when he pushed for the Jones Act with a citizenship clause which was almost certain to delay the day of independence. But in their dealings with the United States, both Muñoz Rivera and Muñoz Marín had made nationhood for Puerto Rico the ultimate goal, and temporary compromises were just that—temporary compromises.

Now, though, Muñoz Marín was beginning to wonder. Independence had a brave ring to it, he must have thought. The very sound of the word could still stir the hearts of the people. But was it really as vital as the elimination of poverty? As full employment? As decent education and the reduction of disease to within acceptable limits? Or wasn't the accomplishment of *these* goals— by any means whatsoever—even more important than independence?

Once in a great while, a man, an idea, and an age appear to be made for each other. It happened in the United States when Franklin D. Roosevelt brought his New Deal program to Washington. It was about to happen in Puerto Rico.

If Muñoz Marín had lived ten or fifteen years earlier— if he had left his party, therefore, ten or fifteen years before he did—he might well have remained just another out-of-power politician. Even as it was, he had a difficult road to travel: His criticism of United States policies had greatly reduced his influence in Washington. The major sources of money in Puerto Rico were firmly ranged against him. When he started, at least, he did not even have a political organization.

Muñoz Marín's split with Antonio R. Barceló over the proposed Tydings Bill of 1936 was blamed by many for the defeat of the Liberal Party in the elections held in that year. This in turn permitted the conservative coalition— made up of the Socialist and Union Republican parties— to remain in power.

All this was not calculated to win Muñoz many friends among those who might have been counted his natural political allies. New Deal liberals, both on the island and in the United States, felt that he had betrayed their cause. As for the conservatives, he had no interest in aligning himself with them, nor, it must be added, they with him.

If Muñoz Marín was still a political leader, in other words, he was the leader of an outvoted and outnumbered faction of an out-of-power party.

By 1937 the break between Muñoz Marín and Barceló was complete, although efforts to reconcile the two factions of the Liberal Party continued for some time after that. In July, 1938, Muñoz put a final end to these efforts by officially announcing the organization of the Popular Democratic Party.

Now that Muñoz had formed his party, however, what was he going to do with it? It was not only broke, but soon lost the only press organ through which it could be sure of presenting its views. *La Democracia*, the newspaper which had been founded by Muñoz' father, was quickly forced into financial difficulties and soon had to suspend publication.

It is true that the Popular Democrats had a great deal of intellectual support. Many university professors and schoolteachers backed it from the beginning. These supporters, however, literally risked losing their jobs if they stuck to their political principles. And in the midst of the Great Depression, this was a very grave risk to run.

But perhaps the most difficult task of all was to fight the built-in apathy and cynicism of the Puerto Rican people. The islanders had been led down too many garden paths to give their trust to anyone easily. They had listened for too many years to too many empty promises: promises from Spain, promises from the United States, promises from their own island leaders. How could they now be expected to take seriously another set of promises from another set of politicians?

A good many observers, during that era, remarked on the apathy and docility of the Puerto Rican people. While a number of outsiders thought of this attitude as "quaint" and "charming," others were both puzzled and worried by it. The 1930 report of the Brookings Institution, for example, stated that "there is a degree of submissiveness and a lack of class feeling that to an outside observer is difficult to understand."

A man such as Muñoz Marín, though, would not be all that puzzled. He was far from an outsider. While he had spent a good deal of time in the United States, he was still a native-born Puerto Rican with his roots firmly planted in island soil. And the fact that his father's name was still venerated on the island gave him a chance to break through the shell of hopelessness and seeming indifference to the core of human passion which lay underneath.

Muñoz took aim at the 1940 elections, therefore, by developing a new style of Puerto Rican political strategy. He had two years available. He used them to travel throughout Puerto Rico—not just the length and breadth of the island, but into the interior as well. Using, for the most part, an ancient automobile, he ignored the typical political banquet circuit and talked face to face and informally with slum dwellers in the cities and *jíbaros* in the mountain country. Since the party had neither a newspaper of its own nor any money for advertising, Muñoz had cars fitted out with loudspeaker systems so that he and his workers could get their message to the people.

The message of the *Populares* was a simple one. The independence issue was ignored as currently unimportant. Social and economic justice, decent living conditions, and better health care and sanitation were among the things that really counted. And if these goals were to be achieved, Muñoz was to insist over and over again, they were going to have to be gained by the Puerto Rican people themselves, and not be handed down, as if from heaven, by the North Americans. The Puerto Ricans, in other words, were going to have to forget about their island's status for a while and use whatever means they had to improve their lot.

The *Populares* did not have the money to bribe the mountain *jíbaros* in the normal and accepted sense—two dollars per vote was the going rate at the time. Nor is it likely that Muñoz Marín would have permitted this practice even if he'd had the cash. He had nothing but contempt for vote-sellers and once compared a man who sells his vote with a *jíbaro* who tosses away his machete in the middle of a fight.

In effect, Muñoz was offering a far more valuable bribe than the contemptuous gift of the price of a few drinks and a square meal. He and his fellow *Populares* were promising to develop a program of more equitable taxation and social services which could make a real improvement in the day-to-day life of the average island-er. The fact that women were voting as well as men (women had actually had the vote in Puerto Rico since 1932, twelve years after the Nineteenth Amendment had been ratified in the continental United States) made this kind of promise even harder to resist.

But the *Populares* still had to overcome the cynicism and distrust of the Puerto Rican people. Muñoz understood that only too well and dealt with the problem frankly. He told his listeners that they were *right* to distrust him. *Never* trust a politician, he would say. What the people should do was examine the program of the Popular Dem-ocrats. If they found that they liked it, they should vote the party into power *without* trusting them. Afterward, they should keep a close check to see how performance measured up to the promised program and, if need be, vote the party out of power again at the next election.

Muñoz Marín swore that if the *Populares* came into power, the party would work for the passage of no less than twenty-two specific laws. It would be an easy matter for the voters to see whether or not that pledge was kept. If the pledge was ignored—or if living conditions were not substantially improved by the program—the voters would be wrong *not* to turn the Popular Democrats out.

Muñoz' campaign made a good deal of sense to the Puerto Rican people. For once they were being treated like responsible adults instead of like little children. The islanders responded by allowing Muñoz to pull off one of the political miracles of modern times. Despite the fact that the *Populares* were in sad need of funds, despite official and unofficial harassment, the Popular Democrats managed to win the 1940 elections.

It was far from an overwhelming victory. Muñoz Marín held only a bare majority—ten out of nineteen seats—in the Senate and two seats less than a majority in the House. But when the Popular Democrats were formed, in 1938, many people did not believe that they would win a single seat in either chamber. Now Muñoz was the president of the Senate and had a fighting chance to push through his program.

Of course there was still no guarantee that the island would benefit. The slogan of the *Populares*—"Bread! Land! Liberty!"—sounded very good on the campaign trail. But sounding good while out of power and being effective while in power are two different things.

In order to get the *Populares'* program off the ground, Muñoz would have to deal with the truculence of the moneyed interests, the jealousy of the island's political establishment, and the real suspicion that the new movement engendered in Washington. To do all this might require an even greater miracle than the winning of the election had.

NINETEEN

LAND REFORM

Washington officials could not have been very pleased about Muñoz Marín's election victory of 1940. Many New Dealers still thought of him as a political opportunist—an irresponsible rabble-rouser and adventurer. There is little doubt that they would have been happier to have a more orthodox leader in power in Puerto Rico.

On the other hand, however, Muñoz was there. He had won. And simply by winning, he managed to symbolize the determination of a growing number of islanders to control their own destinies and to demand what they felt was their due.

But if this were so, another fact was equally obvious. The powers of the federal government had not disappeared. Roosevelt had also just won an election, the one which brought him his unprecedented third term as United States President. And if Muñoz was actually going to accomplish something, he was going to have to work with the Roosevelt administration.

Whatever difficulties this cooperation entailed, though, they were probably more apparent than real. Not only were there men of goodwill on both sides, but—and perhaps more important—political realists. Holding a grudge for past slights—whether real or imagined—is a luxury few politicians are prepared to afford.

Muñoz showed his own grasp of this situation in a letter he wrote to President Roosevelt, congratulating the American leader on his third-term victory. In it, Muñoz

Marín outlined some of his future plans and discussed the policies of the *Populares*.

Roosevelt's answer, as quoted in Earl Parker Hanson's book *Puerto Rico, Land of Wonders* (New York, 1960), included the opinion that "the purposes of the Popular Democratic Party as you have outlined them are highly praiseworthy and should result in vastly improved social and economic conditions for the island. I particularly appreciate your pledge of co-operation," Roosevelt went on, "and assure you that this administration stands ready to do all in its power to assist in finding a solution for the problems of Puerto Rico."

But Muñoz, naturally, was not going to be working with President Roosevelt himself. To a great extent, the success of his program would depend on the goodwill and cooperation of whatever governor would be appointed by Secretary of the Interior Harold L. Ickes. Under the law, the appointed governor still retained the right to veto any bills passed through the Puerto Rican legislature, and the previous governor, Blanton Winship, was well known for his conservative sympathies.

It would have been astounding if Muñoz were not concerned about this. While Secretary Ickes was an absolutely honest man, and while no one could question the sincerity of his desire to help Puerto Rico, his suspicions of militant island leaders had if anything increased in the years that had passed since his outraged reaction to the murder of Colonel Riggs. Muñoz in particular, Ickes believed, had far too many anti-American ideas to be trustworthy.

Still and all, in 1941, after the brief tenures of first Admiral William D. Leahy and then Guy J. Swope, the job of governor was given to the former Brain Truster and undersecretary of agriculture, Rexford Tugwell, who has been both attacked as a socialist and hailed as the finest American governor ever sent to Puerto Rico.

In his inaugural speech, Tugwell pledged himself to work for social progress in specific terms which sounded very much like the terms that Muñoz might have used. But even before he took over his high office, Tugwell had given proof of his desire to cooperate with the *Populares* on such vital matters as land reform.

In 1940 Secretary Ickes had appointed Tugwell to the chairmanship of a committee to study the island's "five-

hundred-acre law." This law was a supplement to the
the original Organic Act of 1900 (the Foraker Act). It
limited the land holdings of any corporation to five hundred acres and, on paper at least, was still in effect.

But the five-hundred-acre section of Foraker did not
have any teeth to it. There were no penalties attached; no
way to enforce it. It had remained a dead issue—although
certainly not a forgotten one in Puerto Rico, at least—
from the time it had been drafted.

The lack of enforcement of the five-hundred-acre section was one of the reasons for Puerto Rico's becoming a
"sugar island" with much of the best land being owned by
a few corporations. By the late thirties, fifty-one corporations owned some 249,000 acres and would often let this
land lie fallow rather than permit it to be used for the
production of food crops.

As early as 1935, the New Deal administration was
showing concern with the tragic results of the no-enforce-
ment policy. Secretary Ickes, in a letter written on January 15 of that year (as quoted in Gordon K. Lewis,
Puerto Rico, Freedom and Power in the Caribbean, New
York, 1963), stated that the island "has been the victim of
the *laissez faire* economy which has developed the rapid
growth of great absentee owned sugar corporations, which
have absorbed much land formerly belonging to small
independent growers and who in consequence have been
reduced to virtual economic serfdom. While the inclusion
of Puerto Rico within our tariff walls has been highly
beneficial to the stockholders of those corporations, the
benefits have not been passed down to the mass of Puerto
Ricans. These on the contrary have seen the lands on
which they formerly raised subsistence crops given over to
sugar production while they have been gradually driven to
import all their food staples, paying for them the high
prices brought about by the tariff."

Some months after this letter was drafted, the newly
appointed attorney general of the island, Benigno Fernández García, was instructed to see whether the five-hundred-acre law could not be legally enforced. On January
28, 1936, therefore, he filed a complaint against a Puerto
Rican corporation, accusing it of holding twelve thousand
acres of land and asking the court to impose a fine and
dissolve the company.

It must have come as a surprise to many Puerto Ricans
that the enforcement attempt was even made. The Roose-

velt-appointed governor, General Blanton Winship, was an anti-reform conservative. Fernández García, however (who was the brother of one of the chief drafters of the Chardón Plan), had the very active help and encouragement of the U.S. Department of the Interior.

The entire sugar industry, well aware of what was at stake, lined up behind the beleaguered defendant, and the island prepared for a bitter court battle. The sugar lawyers had two main contentions: First of all, they maintained that the five-hundred-acre section of Foraker had never been meant to be enforced. If it had been, they said, it would have included some specific provisions for enforcement. Second, since the law had been ignored for such a long time, it would not be fair to enforce it now and thereby penalize those companies who had depended on that fact when they bought land.

It was far from a weak case. Nevertheless, on July 30, 1938, the Supreme Court of Puerto Rico held in favor of the island government.

As was only natural, sugar appealed. On September 27, 1939, the District Court of Appeals in Boston, Massachusetts, reversed that decision, and it appeared as if sugar had won. But the following year, on March 25, 1940, the United States Supreme Court reversed the reversal.

The last word had finally been spoken. It was now official. Puerto Rico could enforce its land laws.

All these events took place before Muñoz Marín and his Popular Democrats were voted into power. Although Muñoz was certainly in favor of enforcing the five-hundred-acre law, he was not one of the principals in the fight to make this possible.

Once in office, however, he attempted to use the five-hundred-acre law in a surprising way. He pushed a bill through the legislature creating a Land Authority through which the Puerto Rican government itself could buy up the land taken away from the sugar industry. Some of this land would be sold, in parcels of no more than twenty-five acres, to small farmers. Other, smaller lots would be given to landless agricultural workers. A large portion of Authority land, however, would continue to produce export crops that were economically profitable. But now the farm laborers would take a fair share of the profits.

Even though the Popular Democrats were able to pass this bill through the legislature, however, that was only half the battle. Guy Swope was now governor of Puerto Rico. The question was, would he sign it?

To help make up his mind, Swope turned to Rexford Tugwell, who was then heading the committee assigned to investigate the law and ways to administer it. The American expert examined the law carefully. Although he did disagree with a few of its points, in the main he liked it and thought that it would benefit the island. Following Tugwell's advice, Governor Swope signed the bill into law.

This was one of the first instances of that close cooperation between Muñoz Marín and Tugwell that was to develop in the next five years. And by means of it, Muñoz was off to a flying start.

The bill which created the Land Authority was more important than even the Puerto Rican leader perhaps guessed. The program of land redistribution was to be a cornerstone of the entire legislative program that was to become associated with his name. It has even been suggested that the economic miracle of "Operation Bootstrap" could not have been possible without that early passage and signing of the Land Authority law.

TWENTY

GOVERNOR TUGWELL

History was moving fast now—both in Puerto Rico and in the outside world.

On the island, the most noteworthy event was the inauguration of Rexford Tugwell as governor. Of course Tugwell used his office to back the Land Authority—which his original encouragement had helped create—as well as other new agencies. But his greatest accomplishments were in the area of training the Puerto Ricans to become more efficient administrators of their own affairs.

Until now the islanders had had little opportunity to run things for themselves. Like most colonial people, they were mainly pushed into the more menial jobs while the mother country supplied the experts who ran the government and the economy. As a result of this, few Puerto Ricans had proper administrative skills. And since human nature is the way it is, most people in the United States felt that Puerto Ricans lacked "natural" drive and ability.

Tugwell set about to change this situation. He himself was a highly experienced administrator. And by the time he was appointed to the governor's job, he had an excellent knowledge of the particular problems of Puerto Rico. He was thus able to teach the *Populares* how to make the creaky and often balky machinery of government work for them in such a way that they could accomplish what they felt had to be done.

Cooperating with the islanders in this manner was no easy task. Furthermore, it brought Tugwell a great deal of criticism from the United States. One Congressman, for example, demanded to know why the governor chose twenty-five-dollar-a-week drugstore clerks and fifteen-hundred-dollar-a-year geography teachers to fill positions as the heads of Puerto Rican agencies.

Whether or not this accusation was exaggerated, however, the Tugwell system appeared to work. During his term of office, the Puerto Ricans set up a number of important new agencies designed to get their island on its feet.

First of all there was the Land Authority itself. A Planning Board was inaugurated to help utilize profits from the sale of nationalized sugar and to help plan for the development of the entire island. Other agencies included a Transportation Authority, a Communications Authority, an island-wide Housing Authority, a Minimum Wage Board, a Development Company, a Development Bank, and a Water Resources Authority.

This proliferation of Puerto Rican government agencies did not bring on the millennium, but it did help to halt the spiral of poverty and misery which had been the island's lot up to that time.

Even as Tugwell was being installed as governor, great events were taking place on the world stage—events that would cast their own shadow over Puerto Rico.

A large part of the world was already at war at the time of his taking office. Then, on December 7, 1941, Japan attacked Pearl Harbor, and the United States and its possessions were embroiled in World War II.

The onset of war meant a number of things to Puerto Rico. First of all, as in World War I, it meant that too many of her sons would die in far-off lands fighting for the United States. Second, it would bring on that old wartime problem of communications and transportation. Puerto Rico was still dependent on the mainland United States both for her basic food supply and as a prime market for her products, and German submarines were doing their best to cut the vital shipping lanes.

One big question mark was what would happen to social progress. Puerto Rico was the keystone of the American defense system in the Caribbean, and Tugwell's first duty was to help shape its military function and to prepare for possible attack on the exposed and isolated island. A great many people would say, "Win the war first—then talk about better conditions." Would Tugwell listen to them?

Tugwell did not listen—although at times he must have been tempted to do so.

One rather surprising problem which World War II brought in its wake was that of rising unemployment.

In the continental United States, the war created new jobs and helped bring an end to the Great Depression. But then, in the United States, peacetime manufacturing industries could be quickly turned toward war work—automobile plants, for example, were transformed into aircraft factories. Puerto Rico, on the other hand, did not have this kind of industrial setup to begin with. The industries she did have—such as needlework or citrus fruit—were sadly damaged by lack of transport.

One industry which was greatly helped by the war, however, was the rum industry. When the production of liquor in the United States became a wartime casualty, Puerto Rican rum was eagerly consumed in its place. Much of the social progress that was made during the war years, indeed, would not have been possible without the newly prosperous rum industry and the large sums of tax money it brought to the island.

While all this was going on, Governor Tugwell was making powerful enemies both in Puerto Rico and in Washington. The wealthy class on the island, resentful of many of the new changes, combined with conservatives in both houses of Congress in making attacks on his patriotism and his political philosophy.

In the year 1943 both the House and the Senate sent investigating subcommittees to Puerto Rico in order to look into charges that a great socialistic and anti-American conspiracy existed there under Tugwell's protection. The fact that the insular government was now owning and operating power systems, sugar factories, and the like was taken as evidence that its leaders were conspiring to create a Red dictatorship.

Those who backed the new programs met these charges by stating that—in wartime especially—a sullen, ill-fed, and discontented population was an active danger to the mother country. Social improvement, they said in partial answer to the "win the war first" argument, was not only morally right but necessary to the war effort. Muñoz

Marín himself used to say that the *Populares* were neither radical nor conservative: they were realistic.

The respectability of the *Populares'* program did get one boost when an old political enemy of Tugwell's, the conservative Senator Robert A. Taft, came to the island with a Senate subcommittee and later expressed himself as favoring much of what the Puerto Ricans were doing. In a letter to the chairman of the U.S. War Production Board concerning a new glass factory that was being financed as well as owned by the island government, Taft stated: "I have never been very strong for government-supported industry, but the situation in Puerto Rico is such that I believe the government has a proper function in promoting the development of new industry."

The voters of Puerto Rico had a chance to show their feelings toward the programs of the Popular Democrats in the 1944 elections. The results of this could not be misread. In 1940 the *Populares* had won by a whisker; now they swept into office by a landslide. Instead of holding the bare majority of 10 out of the 19 Senate seats, they held no less than 17. Instead of holding 18 of the 39 seats in the House of Representatives, they managed to garner 37.

Although there was no doubt now that Muñoz' program had the backing of the island, its enemies did not go away. In Washington, indeed, they grew more vocal. And since they could not do anything about Muñoz and the other elected Popular Democrats, they concentrated their anger on the appointed governor, even presenting bills in Congress to try and force Tugwell's removal.

In 1946, with the war successfully ended, the Republicans captured control of the U.S. Congress. Faced with the hostility of the resurgent conservatives, Tugwell realized that his continued presence on the island would be actually harmful to island progress.

When Tugwell resigned, however, he was able to perform one more service to the island. He persuaded President Harry Truman to appoint a native Puerto Rican, Jesús Piñero, as his successor.

Rexford Tugwell, to repeat, has been called the best American governor in Puerto Rico's history. It is also true, however, that he was the object of much resentment and criticism on the island—not merely from hidebound conservatives and people with a vested interest in the status quo, but from many of the *Populares* themselves.

Tugwell's positive qualities are obvious. His integrity, his goodwill, his courage in the face of powerful opposition, and his determination to do what was right cannot be questioned. Some observers, on the other hand, accuse him of that subtle sin of colonialism, and of forgetting that it was the "natives"—in this case Muñoz Marín and his fellow *Populares*—who actually designed the new programs that took effect during his tenure as governor.

Gordon K. Lewis, in his *Puerto Rico, Freedom and Power in the Caribbean* (New York, 1963), writes: "It is not too much to say that the Governor saw the whole scene in terms of another Rooseveltian drama in which he played the role of the President and Muñoz, as it were, that of Speaker Sam Rayburn, without ever fully appreciating that the genius of Muñoz made such an allocation of roles fantastically unrealistic."

Another writer—Earl Parker Hanson, in his book *Puerto Rico, Land of Wonders* (New York, 1960)—remarks that "Tugwell seems not to have realized that he was not the designer of Puerto Rico's new program, was *not* the great leader whose task it was to define, explore, and chart new paths for the island's salvation."

Actually, as Hanson goes on to state, it was the Puerto Ricans themselves who had worked out the new paths which the island was now exploring. Muñoz Marín began formulating his ideas as far back as 1920 when he was living in New York. Other Puerto Rican intellectuals and professionals helped him to modify and sharpen his thinking in the years that followed. Tugwell's basic function as governor, Hanson insists, was "to lend his sturdy help and administrative experience to the task of following paths that had long since been charted by others."

If this was Tugwell's attitude, there is little wonder that it caused resentment among the *Populares*. And the resentment only deepened when, in 1947, the former governor published a book about his Puerto Rican experiences. The book was called *The Stricken Land*. But according to Hanson, many Puerto Ricans felt that it would have been better titled *The Stricken Rexford*.

Despite any flaws, though, Tugwell performed a necessary function on the island. If it were not for his active cooperation, the program of the *Populares* would have had a much more difficult time being made into law—

that is, if it could have been made into law at all. And even more important than that, he taught the islanders the administrative skills that they would so desperately need in just a few years' time.

TWENTY-ONE

COMMONWEALTH AND *FOMENTO*

The wartime partnership of Tugwell and Muñoz Marín may be credited with two major accomplishments: It prevented the problems of the island from becoming any worse than they had been, and it created a strong base from which to take further action.

By 1945, however, it had become clear that the situation on the island was not substantially improving. The growth of most industries—sugar, tobacco, coffee, and the like—had come to a virtual standstill. Only the rum industry seemed to be still on the way up.

For Muñoz and the other Puerto Rican leaders, it was a time to take stock. What were Puerto Rico's assets and liabilities? How would it be possible to promote rapid economic growth in a land that had always been poor?

The result of this period of stock-taking was a program that has become known in the United States and throughout the world as Operation Bootstrap, and on the island itself as *Fomento* (a word which can be roughly translated as "development"). It may be a mistake to claim, as some enthusiasts have, that *Fomento* has transformed Puerto Rico into an economic and sociological paradise. But there is no doubt that the program has made a tremendous difference in the life of the island and its ordinary people.

Operation Bootstrap can trace the roots of its history back to the Puerto Rico Industrial Development Company, an agency which the government founded in 1942 in order to help establish new factories. During and after the war PRIDCO was greatly expanded and the construction of new plants on the island increased.

At about this time, Muñoz Marín and other Popular Democratic leaders concluded that one of the strongest assets that Puerto Rico did have was her freedom from certain United States taxes, including the federal income tax. This had come about because Puerto Rico—not being a state—had no voice in national election.

For years the tax break had been a boon to wealthy individuals and to corporations that were based on the island. Now the Puerto Rican leaders decided to use it as an inducement to attract the kind of industrial enterprise that the island needed. To sweeten the deal still further, they would offer to delay the imposition of all local income taxes for a given number of years.

The plan appeared to be workable. Why shouldn't new industries flock to the island under these conditions? For the first ten years or more of their stay in Puerto Rico—depending on the specific case—they would be free from all income taxes plus, it was decided, most other taxes as well. And even after a company had exhausted its years of local tax exemption, it would find that it had to pay far less on the island than it would if it had built its plant in the continental United States. Furthermore, because of the island's economic history, there was no question but that Puerto Rican labor could be purchased at a lower cost.

But a major corporation—that is, the kind of healthy corporation which Muñoz and the others wanted—would demand something more than cheap labor and a good tax break before it would take the risk of investing its money in Puerto Rico. It would want proper conditions: an alert and well-trained work force, a modern transportation network, sufficient power to meet its needs, and all the other things that help make industry prosper.

Because of the start made during the Tugwell years, Puerto Rico could now supply most of these demands. And what the island didn't have, it set about getting. Programs to promote health and vocational training, for example, were broadened in scope.

On July 1, 1950, *Fomento* was expanded and reorganized. The program now included three major sections: the original PRIDCO, which would concentrate on real estate and certain specialized financial functions; a Puerto

Rico Ports Authority, which would be in charge of the island's ports; and the Economic Development Administration, which would devote itself to industrial promotion and the promotion of tourism.

Operation Bootstrap was under way.

While these economic developments were taking place, Puerto Rico was also undergoing enormous political changes. The first of these, a harbinger of things to come, took place in 1947, when the American Congress decided to amend the Jones Act in order to permit Puerto Rico to elect a governor who would then appoint his own cabinet.

This had to be a vast improvement. Tugwell's successor, Jesús Piñero, was a good governor, a native Puerto Rican, and—as one of the founders of the majority Popular Democratic Party—was anxious to cooperate with the island's elected leaders. Still and all, he was appointed by Washington and thus fundamentally responsible to the federal government. Now, though, Puerto Rico's internal affairs were to be truly in the hands of its own citizens. This was to be the first time one could make that statement since 1493, when Christopher Columbus landed on Boriquen.

An election for governor was called for 1948. Muñoz Marín ran for the office. He decided to make the campaign a test for a new way—or rather an updating of an old way—to solve the question of the island's status. Muñoz had now come to believe that this could be best done neither through statehood nor independence, but through a third choice called commonwealth.

Should Puerto Rico become independent, Muñoz pointed out, islanders would forego their American citizenship and the island would no longer be under the social, economic, and military protection of the United States. Should it become a state, on the other hand, Puerto Rico would lose its important tax advantages—a situation which could bring grave economic harm. Choosing the status of commonwealth would mean avoiding the penalties while, at the same time, raising Puerto Rico from its humiliating colonial role. The island would be a self-governing, autonomous entity keeping voluntarily within the American system.

An *autonomous* entity? Yes. Muñoz Marín had reached back in history to the ideas of the Puerto Rican Autonomists of the late nineteenth century. What he was calling for now was something very similar to the agreement which his father, Muñoz Rivera, had signed with Spain shortly before the American invasion of 1898.

Once again, the Popular Democrats won in a landslide. Muñoz Marín himself garnered 61 per cent of the vote for governor. The United States took this victory as a show of approval for Muñoz' ideas. In July of 1950 the American Congress passed a law permitting Puerto Rico to draft its own constitution.

Things were happening fast. Political problems which had remained in status quo for far too many years were now being settled with astonishing swiftness.

In Puerto Rico a Constitutional Assembly was elected. This Assembly drafted a document along the lines that Muñoz had proposed. The commonwealth constitution was put to the people in the referendum of 1951, and more than 76 per cent of them voted for it. The following year, on July 25, 1952—a date which fell on the fifty-fourth anniversary of the landing of American troops—commonwealth status was proclaimed.

The long colonial era had finally come to an end. The era of commonwealth and *Fomento* was at hand.

TWENTY-TWO

YESTERDAY, TODAY, AND TOMORROW

As I write these words, Puerto Rico has been a commonwealth for a little more than eighteen years. The *Fomento* program has been in existence for some time longer.

The changes that have come over the island in this period have been nothing less than amazing. New factories have been built, new industries started, and the economy has made steady gains. From the time of its inception through 1968, the island's Economic Development Administration has attracted more than 1,700 manufacturing plants to Puerto Rico. This represents a private, fixed investment of about $1.2 billion. In 1968 alone, 226 new ventures were promoted.

All this industrial progress means that more and more of Puerto Rico's burgeoning work force can be employed. Taking the year 1968 again—which was the last year for which figures are now generally available—more than 100,000 islanders were employed in EDA-promoted plants alone.

Not too terribly long ago, Puerto Rico was a single-crop, agricultural island. Today it receives its income in a variety of ways. In 1968, net income from manufacturing was more than $750 million, net income from the construction industry was $250 million, while tourism—which got its postwar start with the building of the Caribe Hilton in 1949 and bounded upward with the coming of the jet age—brought in a total net of $202 million. Of course agriculture itself was still bringing in money. Total farm output during 1968 was more than $267 billion.

Despite these impressive facts and figures, however, things on the island are still far from perfect. Unemployment still hovers at betwen 11 to 12 per cent of the work force. And per capita yearly income was only $1,129 in 1968—a great improvement over the per capita income of $120 in 1940, but a long way from acceptability.

If more evidence is needed of Puerto Rico's continuing social and financial troubles, it can be found in the vast number of islanders who have left in order to try and make a better living in New York City and other places in the continental United States. This exodus began after World War II, and by 1968 well over half a million Puerto Ricans had made the northward trip. Their heartbreaking problems of readjustment are outside the scope of this book and have been amply related elsewhere.

The island's political situation has not been notably serene either, in the years since the commonwealth was born. If Muñoz Marín thought that he had finally settled the issue of statehood versus independence versus some sort of autonomy, he was very much mistaken. There is still a large pro-statehood movement on the island as well as a small, though highly vocal, movement toward complete independence.

On November 1, 1950, a group of pro-independence fanatics attempted to assassinate President Harry Truman in the United States. Less than four years later, on March 1, 1954, several members of the extremist Nationalist Party made their way into the House of Representatives in Washington, where they shot and wounded five Congressmen. Although these violent episodes served mainly to discredit the pro-independence cause, talk about it did not cease—either on the island itself or in Puerto Rican colonies which have grown up in such cities as New York.

But of the two noncommonwealth solutions, statehood was by far the more popular. By 1962, indeed, a strong feeling for statehood was making itself felt.

In August of 1964, a political bombshell was dropped on Puerto Rico. Luis Muñoz Marín, now more than sixty-six years of age, announced that he would not run for another term as governor.

Muñoz had already been elected to four terms as the island's chief executive. And few doubt that he could have held on to the office for as long as he wished. But he had been active in Puerto Rican politics since the 1920's and had been the most powerful political leader on the island since the *Populares'* victory of 1940. That was enough. Explaining that he felt it was dangerous to keep any man in power for too long, he could not be dissuaded from leaving the governorship and running for the Senate.

The Popular Democratic candidate for governor in the 1964 elections was Roberto Sánchez Vilella, a long-time associate of Muñoz and his chosen successor. Sánchez won his election, and the *Populares*—Muñoz among them—once more took control of the legislature.

In that same year a commission was appointed to study the old, nagging problem of the island's future status. The commission report backed the *Populares'* position. It would be at least twenty-five more years, it found, before Puerto Rico would be in a healthy enough economic condition to be ready for statehood. It would take even longer for the island to be ready to meet independence.

This report was not universally accepted in Puerto Rico. And in July of 1967, a new plebiscite was given to the people. When the vote was counted, about 60 per cent had opted to continue with the commonwealth, some 39 per cent preferred statehood, while less than 1 per cent of those voting selected independence.

The results seemed clear-cut. Despite the vehemence and articulateness with which they put their case, the pro-independence faction had little support on the island. But there was a growing sentiment in favor of statehood.

During the four years of the Sánchez administration, relations between the governor and Muñoz Marín became strained. Sánchez decided to leave Muñoz' Popular Democratic Party and form a new party, the People's Party, which he led.

In the meantime, the major opposition party, the Statehood Republican Party, was also having its troubles. Luis A. Ferré, a businessman-politician who had been the party's three-time candidate for governor, was battling the leadership over the 1967 plebiscite issue. Ferré, a strong statehood advocate, believed that the island's status could only be settled by such a plebiscite and was urging his party to lead the fight for statehood during that referendum. When the party decided to remain aloof, Ferré dropped out to organize the United Statehooders Association.

About one month after the plebiscite was held, the United Statehooders organized the frankly political New Progressive Party with Ferré as its president.

The gubernatorial election of 1968 was basically a three-way fight. The Popular Democrats refused to renominate Governor Sánchez Vilella and chose, instead, the Senate majority leader Luis Negrón López. Sánchez made his own bid for reelection under the banner of the People's Party, while the New Progressive Party went with Ferré. The upshot was that Ferré won with 44.6 per cent of the total vote cast. Negrón received 42.1 per cent, while Sánchez ended up with 9.9 per cent.

Governor Ferré, incidentally, is still very much in favor of eventual statehood for Puerto Rico. He believes that commonwealth status is serving as a middle step on the way to statehood.

It would take a brave man to predict today which course Puerto Rico will eventually follow with regard to its political status. Although the majority of Puerto Ricans still appear to favor their island's remaining a commonwealth, we have already seen that sentiment for statehood is on the increase. And one cannot completely write off a shift of opinion in favor of independence. Vocal minorities, even very tiny ones, have been known to end up carrying the day.

But the issue of the island's status is only the most dramatic question mark in Puerto Rico's future. It would be just as hard to predict the political futures of the different leaders there.

After many years of domination by the Popular Democratic Party, island politics are once more in ferment. New political parties have been springing up, and it even remains to be seen if the *Populares* movement can be held together by the brilliant personality of the aging Muñoz Marín.

Looking at where Puerto Rico has come from, however, and seeing the distance she has traveled in comparison with her Caribbean neighbors, it is hard not to be an optimist. During the decade between 1958 and 1968, for example, Puerto Rico's gross national product increased on an average of 7.5 per cent a year—which is far higher than the norm, not only for the Caribbean, but for both underdeveloped and industrialized nations throughout the world. Ironically, the chances are that sentiment for statehood would not have grown so fast if a certain amount of prosperity had not taken place under the Commonwealth.

All we have to judge anything by is the past. And judging by the past, Puerto Rico can and will solve her problems. The question marks all have to do with methods.

The future remains cloudy. But whatever path Puerto Rico chooses, she will have a future. And most probably a good one.

Author's addendum:

On November 3, 1972, while this book was being readied for publication, a new election was held in Puerto Rico. Governor Ferré and his pro-statehood forces were defeated. The new governor, Rafael Hernandez Colon, is a member of the Popular Democratic Party, which is now back in power after an absence of four years.

—M. J. G.
February, 1973

Sources in English

One of the major purposes of this book is to encourage English-speaking readers to dig further into the subject of Puerto Rico and its history. Any reader who does this, however, will face the problem of finding English-language sources. There is such a shameful lack of this material available that a cynic might even consider it as another instance of American neglect. My own book, indeed, is the only general, popular history of the island to be addressed to English-speaking adults in recent years.

I hope that this situation will change. It would please me greatly if by the time these words are read they will no longer be true. It may even be that some of the fine history books that have been written in Spanish will be available in English translation.

In the meantime, though—just in case this millennium does not come to pass—I am offering a list of some of the English-language books which I have found helpful along with my own comments when appropriate.

BANNON, JOHN FRANCIS, *Indian Labor in the Spanish Indies*. Boston, 1966. Bound in paper as part of the D. C. Heath and Company series "Problems in Latin American Civilization," the book is an anthology of different viewpoints concerning the Spanish treatment of native labor in the New World. It is not only useful, but generally available.

BERBUSSE, EDWARD J., *The United States in Puerto Rico, 1898–1900*. Chapel Hill, 1966. A minute examination of this critical period.

BOWEN, J. DAVID, *The Island of Puerto Rico*. Philadelphia 1968. Published as part of Lippincott's "Portraits of the Na tions" series, the book is apparently aimed at high school students. While not a history as such, it does contain historical information.

BRAU, M. M., *Island in the Crossroads*. New York, 1968. A history of the island written specifically for "young people" and bound in paper.

FERNÁNDEZ MÉNDEZ, EUGENIO, *The Sources on Puerto Rican Culture History*. San Juan, 1967. A fifty-five-page booklet which critically appraises historical works written in both Spanish and English. This monograph is a wonderfully valuable bibliographical tool, but is extremely hard to obtain. I found my personal copy in a little shop in San Juan, but do not know if any more are available either on the island or in the United States.

FLINTER, JOHN D., *An Account of the Present State of Puerto Rico*. London, 1834. Colonel Flinter came to the island in the service of the Spanish crown. He was a shrewd and sharp-eyed observer.

GRUBER, RUTH, *Puerto Rico, Island of Promise*. New York, 1960. A descriptive book by a trained newspaper correspondent which also contains two historical chapters.

HANCOCK, RALPH, *Puerto Rico, A Traveler's Guide*. Princeton, 1962. Published as a guide book, it actually holds a tremendous amount of information—including historical information—on Puerto Rico. This information is arranged alphabetically under headings, which makes it an extremely handy reference book.

HANSON, EARL PARKER, *Puerto Rico, Land of Wonders*. New York, 1960. This book concentrates mainly on the era of Muñoz Marín. Since Parker knows that era intimately, he gives an authentic if enthusiastic portrait of it.

HARING, C. H., *The Spanish Empire in America*. New York, 1947. A scholarly discussion of the Spanish system of colonial government.

ICKES, HAROLD L., *The Secret Diary of Harold L. Ickes, The First Thousand Days*. New York, 1953. Some information on Puerto Rico in the days of the New Deal.

LEWIS, GORDON K., *Puerto Rico, Freedom and Power in the Caribbean*. New York, 1963. A long and detailed socio-economic study of the island concentrating mainly on the latter part of the American era. It contains much historical information.

MIXER, KNOWLTON, *Porto Rico, History and Conditions.* New York, 1926. A history which reflects the "enlightened" attitudes of the American colonial period.

MORALES CARRIÓN, ARTURO, *Puerto Rico and the Non-Hispanic Caribbean.* San Juan, 1953. This book, which Eugenio Fernández Méndez calls "the most serious and scholarly work yet published on a Puerto Rican theme," examines the period between 1493 and 1815. The book, unfortunately, is not easily available in the United States, although there are copies in the American History Collection of the New York Public Library and in other major libraries. Dr. Morales Carrión has indicated plans eventually to publish a continuation of his work in order to take his study to the modern era.

MORISON, SAMUEL ELIOT, *Admiral of the Ocean Sea.* Boston, 1942. A biography of Christopher Columbus which also contains some useful information concerning the Taino and Carib Indians.

PUERTO RICO RECONSTRUCTION ADMINISTRATION, *Puerto Rico, A Guide to the Island of Boriquén.* New York, 1940. This book was sponsored by the Puerto Rico Department of Education and contains a short historical section plus a concise summary of the island's political parties from 1866 to the time of writing.

STERLING, PHILIP, and BRAU, MARÍA, *The Quiet Rebels.* New York, 1968. Written for "young people," this contains four biographies of Puerto Rican historical figures: Muñoz, father and son; José C. Barbosa; José de Diego.

TIME-LIFE LIBRARY, *The U. S. Overseas.* New York, 1969. The section on Puerto Rico contains a good condensed history of the island.

TUGWELL, REXFORD G., *The Stricken Land.* New York, 1947. Tugwell's own version of his time as governor of Puerto Rico.

VAN MIDDELDYK, R. A., *The History of Puerto Rico from the Spanish Discovery to the American Occupation,* edited by Martin G. Brumbaugh. New York, 1902. Despite its age and what appear to be occasional inaccuracies, this book remains an interesting and useful recounting of the Spanish period.

Index

MENTOR Books of Special Interest

☐ **PREJUDICE: TWENTY TALES OF OPPRESSION AND LIBERATION edited by Charles R. Larson.** The twenty stories in this powerful anthology have one common theme as their concern—racial prejudice. The writers represent ten different countries. Included are **Albert Camus, Flannery O'Connor** and **Anatole France.** A biographical sketch of each author is included.

(#MW1070—$1.50)

☐ **THE CHICANO: FROM CARICATURE TO SELF-PORTRAIT edited and with an Introduction by Edward Simmen.** An anthology of short stories offering for the first time a collection of writings devoted exclusively to the Mexican-American. These stories often comic, sometimes tragic —present the Mexican-American as an individual caught in a social order that demands he meet that society on its own terms—or suffer. Among the writers included are Bret Harte, Jack London, and Genaro Gonzalez.

(#MW1069—$1.50)

☐ **LATIN AMERICA: MYTH AND REALITY by Peter Nehemkis.** An attempt to unmask the mythology that blocks understanding of Latin Americans by North Americans, and of North Americans by Latin Americans. "A perceptive and thoughtful examination of contemporary Latin America—its institutional, economic and political image and its reality."—**Foreign Affairs** Magazine

(#MY958—$1.25)

☐ **FIVE FAMILIES by Oscar Lewis.** An intimate and objective study of a typical day in the lives of five Mexican families. A great anthropological study by an expert in the field of Mexican studies. (#MQ658—95¢)

SIGNET and MENTOR Books You'll Want to Read

☐ **CHILD OF THE DARK: THE DIARY OF CAROLINA DE JESUS** translated by David St. Clair. A woman's vivid diary of her daily struggle for survival in a squalid Brazilian slum. "One of the most astonishing documents of the lower depths ever printed."—Newsweek. Illustrated with photographs. (#Y5685—$1.25)

☐ **DOES FIDEL EAT MORE THAN YOUR FATHER?** Conversations in Cuba by Barry Reckord. "Third world view" of Castro's Cuba by a young Jamaican writer. "Illuminating . . ."—New York Times Book Review
(#Q5130—95¢)

☐ **THE GUERRILLAS** by Jean Lartéguy. This is the story of a seven-month journalistic tour of the Latin American continent and of Jean Lartéguy's search for the truth about Che Guevara. "His descriptions ring, and his historical allusions illuminate the present moment like sudden skyborne flares."—Book Guide
(#Y5060—$1.25)

☐ **PAIN AND PROMISE: THE CHICANO TODAY** edited and with an Introduction by Edward Simmen. Thirty-two essays on the dramatic emergence of the Mexican-American from passive endurance of century-old indifference and injustice at the hands of Anglo society. Included are essays by César Chávez, José Angel Gutíerrez, Reies Lopez Tijerina and Philip D. Ortego.
(#MY1139—$1.25)

NEW AMERICAN LIBRARY PUBLISHES SIGNET, SIGNETTE, MENTOR, CLASSIC, PLUME & NAL BOOKS

MENTOR
BOOK

A SHORT HISTORY OF
PUERTO
RICO

The story of Puerto Rico begins far back in time—
perhaps a hundred million years ago—when it was
part of a huge land mass that now makes up
the group of islands including Jamaica, Hispaniola,
Cuba, and Puerto Rico. Author Morton J. Golding
begins his study of this "island in the sun" long
after the advent of its second geological life, during
the period of Puerto Rico's first inhabitants, the
primitive, peaceful Siboney Indians. His account of
the island's history moves from its takeover by
the more civilized Taino Indians in the thirteenth
century, through the landing of Columbus, the
subsequent Spanish rule and later American intervention, to present-day Puerto Rican politics and
the island's drive toward statehood. Written with
great empathy, *A Short History of Puerto Rico*
is the product of extensive research, including
lengthy discussions with scholars of Puerto Rican
culture and history. It examines Puerto Rico from
cultural, geographical, and political standpoints
and is the only general, popular history of the
island written for English-speaking adults in
recent years.

5590

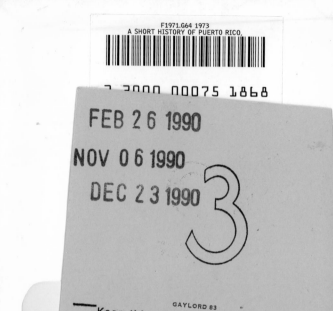